Mozart

PRODIGY OF NATUR

C A BANKS AND J RIGBIE TURNER

PRODIGY OF NATURE

THE PIERPONT MORGAN LIBRARY

NEW YORK

THE BRITISH LIBRARY

LONDON

1991

This book is published on the occasion of the exhibition
Mozart: 'Prodigy of Nature'
commemorating the bicentennial of the death of
Wolfgang Amadeus Mozart
(27 January 1756 – 5 December 1791)

The Pierpont Morgan Library, New York. 8 May – 4 August 1991
The British Library, London. 30 August – 12 January 1992
The exhibition has been sponsored by J.P. Morgan & Co. Incorporated

©1991 C A Banks and J Rigbie Turner
First published 1991 jointly by The Pierpont Morgan Library, New York
and The British Library, London
ISBN 0 8759 8092 9 (Pierpont Morgan Library)
ISBN 0 7123 0240 9 (British Library)
Library of Congress Catalog Card Number 91 – 60048
British Library Cataloguing in Publication Data
Banks, C. A.
Mozart: prodigy of nature.
1. Austria. Music
I. Title II. Turner, J. Rigbie
780.92

Frontispiece: detail from the trio of Mozart's String Quartet in D major, K.575.
[The British Library: Department of Manuscripts – Add. MS 37765]

Map (page 10) by John Mitchell
Designed and typeset on Ventura in Palatino by Roger Davies
Printed in England
on 135 gm^2 Appledawn Cream Velvet long-life paper
by BAS Printers, Over Wallop, Hampshire

Contents

I leave the matter to the grace of God. It depends on His grace whether He wishes to keep this prodigy of nature in the world in which he has placed it, or to take it to Himself. I shall certainly watch over it so well that it is all one whether we are in Salzburg or in any other part of the world. But it is this watching which makes travelling expensive.

Leopold Mozart in February 1764 following the suggestion that Mozart be inoculated against smallpox.

Foreword

In 1991 we commemorate the bicentennial of the death of one of the greatest composers of all time, Wolfgang Amadeus Mozart. The circumstances of his life and death, combined with the depth and immediacy of his music, have caught the public imagination as has happened with perhaps only one other composer, Beethoven. Through his music Mozart's spirit is still very much alive today. The fact that his music is so widely performed is due to public demand; the fact that his music *can* be widely performed is ultimately due to the libraries that have preserved and made available a multitude of important editions — the entries for Mozart take up 204 2-column pages in The British Library's music catalogue — and, above all, the autograph scores on which all publication of Mozart's music must depend. One has only to read the newspapers after the public sale of a Mozart autograph to see how highly they are prized in financial terms.

Since both The British Library and The Pierpont Morgan Library are fortunate enough to possess superb collections of Mozart autograph manuscripts it was natural that each should decide to mount a major exhibition to celebrate Mozart's bicentenary. By great good fortune J.P. Morgan & Co. Incorporated offered to sponsor an exhibition combining the best of both collections to be shown in New York and London during the bicentenary year. Our immediate debt of gratitude is therefore to the Chairman and Board of the Bank for making this splendid joint project possible. In particular we should like to thank Mr Frederick H. S. Allen, Vice-President, Corporate Communication–Europe, at the Bank for the close interest he as representative of the sponsor has personally taken in every aspect of the exhibition. His support in our planning has been invaluable.

Our next expression of gratitude is to Mrs Chris Banks and Mr J. Rigbie Turner, curators in The British Library Music Library and The Pierpont Morgan Library respectively, who have planned the exhibitions and written this accompanying book.

All parties agreed early on that an exhibition could appropriately be built upon autographs from the libraries' collections, augmented by others which could be borrowed from close to hand and enhanced visually by use of graphic materials, pictures and musical instruments. We are therefore very grateful to the following lenders:

New York Exhibition: Mr James J. Fuld, Mr Robert Owen Lehman, the Frederick R. Koch Foundation, Department of Musical Instruments of The Metropolitan Museum of Art, The Houghton Library of Harvard University, Mr Maurice Sendak, Geography and Map Division, The Library of Congress; Music Division, The New York Public Library at Lincoln Center, Astor, Lenox and Tilden Foundations.

The exhibition is supported by an indemnity from the Federal Council on the Arts and Humanities.

London exhibition: HM The Queen, The Administrateur Géneral of the Bibliothèque Nationale, Paris, His Grace the Duke of Atholl, The Trustees of the British Museum, Cambridge University Library, Mr Alec Cobbe, The Governors of Dulwich Picture Gallery, Glasgow University Library, The Trustees of the National Portrait Gallery, Mr Albi Rosenthal, The Board of the Royal Academy of Music, The Board of the Royal College of Music.

There is, however, perhaps a deeper debt to be acknowledged. Each Library is in the possession of its collection because of acts of generosity on the part of individual donors. In 1910 Harriet Chichele Plowden bequeathed to the British Museum (forerunner of The British Library) the scores of all ten of Mozart's mature string quartets and in 1986 the Trustees of the Stefan Zweig Collection generously gave his superb collection of literary and musical autographs to The British Library, including sixteen Mozart autographs of which the famous autograph thematic catalogue is one of the highlights of this exhibition. The Pierpont Morgan Library is deeply indebted to the Trustees of the Mary Flagler Cary Charitable Trust who, in 1968, gave the Morgan Library Mrs Cary's extraordinary collection of music manuscripts and letters and, who, over the past twenty-three years, have made possible the purchase of many manuscripts of Mozart and other composers; to the Heineman Foundation which, in 1977, gave the Morgan Library the Dannie and Hettie Heineman Collection, which contains several major Mozart manuscripts and important Mozart letters; to Robert Owen Lehman, whose superb collection of music manuscripts has been on deposit in the Library since 1972; and to the Frederick R. Koch Foundation, whose collection is also on deposit, and whose purchases in the 1980's have substantially enriched the Library's holdings. Without the altruism of all these donors and their willingness to ensure that the general public should be able to enjoy these priceless treasures in perpetuity, this exhibition would not have been possible.

As it is, Mozart: 'Prodigy of Nature' stands as evidence of the international co-operation between two great libraries, and is surely a fitting tribute to a composer whose music has transcended all language barriers and international boundaries.

J MICHAEL SMETHURST
DIRECTOR GENERAL
HUMANITIES & SOCIAL SCIENCES
THE BRITISH LIBRARY

CHARLES E PIERCE JR
DIRECTOR
THE PIERPONT MORGAN LIBRARY

Acknowledgements

In addition to the people mentioned in the Foreword the authors would like to extend their thanks to all those who have assisted in many different ways at every stage in the preparation of the exhibition and this accompanying book. In particular we would like to thank the following: John Arthur, David Avery, Evan Baker, Paul Banks, Richard Chesser, Hugh Cobbe, Susan E. Eley, Timothy Herstein, Shelley Jones, Alec Hyatt King, David A. Loggie, Laurence Libin, Kathleen Luhrs, Hope Mayo, O. W. Neighbour, Virginia Nelson, Patricia Reyes, Stanley Sadie, Arthur Searle, Nancy Seaton, Edward J. Sowinsky, Alan Sterenberg, Alan Tyson, David Way, Elizabeth Wilson, Fredric Woodbridge Wilson, David W. Wright and colleagues at The British Library, London, and The Pierpont Morgan Library, New York.

In addition we are extremely grateful to the Macmillan Press Limited for permitting us to use excerpts from *The Letters of Mozart and his Family* in the translation by Emily Anderson.

For permission to reproduce illustrations of items in collections other than those in The British Library and The Pierpont Morgan Library thanks are due to the following: HM The Queen; the Trustees of the British Museum; the Governors of Dulwich Picture Gallery; the Administrateur Géneral of the Bibliothèque Nationale, Paris; the Librarian, Glasgow University Library.

ENGLAND

London

Dover

Calais
Dunkirk

UNITED
PROVINCES

The Hague

Antwerp
Brussels

AUSTRIAN
NETHERLANDS

Aachen
Cologne
Coblenz

Mainz

Rhine

PRUSSIA

POLAND

Berlin

HOLY ROMAN EMPIRE

BOHEMIA

Prague

Brno

Frankfurt am Main

Mannheim
Heidelberg

AUSTRIA

Vienna

Seine

Versailles
Paris

Strasbourg

Augsburg

Munich

Passau
Linz

Danube

Salzburg

FRANCE

Zurich

SWITZERLAND

Lausanne

Geneva

Innsbruck

HUNGARY

Bolzano

Milan
Cremona

Verona
Padua
Mantua

Venice

Parma
Bologna

Florence

Siena

ITALY

Rome

Naples

0   100   200   *miles*   300

0   100   200   300   *kms*

Europe in Mozart's time

Introduction

LEOPOLD MOZART recognised his son's extraordinary musical talents at an early stage and sought to bring them to the attention of a wide and influential audience. At the same time, he ensured that an account would be kept of his son's development and experiences by recording many of them in letters and journals and by encouraging members of his family to do likewise. It is clear from some of these letters that Leopold persuaded the recipients to keep them: to his wife he wrote 'I hope that you are carefully collecting all our letters' (from Milan in 1770) and later in 1773 he indicated to her that she should remove the final portion of a letter 'so that it may not fall into the hands of others' — a wish which Frau Mozart did not carry out.

The correspondence continued between father and son when the two were apart and reveal much of Mozart's own aspirations, working methods and lifestyle, as well as his father's thoughts on how his son should be conducting his life. The surviving letters contain abundant information about Mozart's life, particularly his early development, and we have used them to provide much of the commentary in the exhibition and in this book.

Precisely because such a substantial record exists it has been necessary to limit the present volume to a narrative which highlights and places into context some of the items included in the exhibition, many of which are illustrated here. We hope that by following the travels of Mozart and his family from his childhood home in Salzburg to his adopted one in Vienna, we have provided a narrative that is both of general interest to the Mozart enthusiast and that serves as a permanent record for those who visit the exhibition.

CHRIS BANKS & J RIGBIE TURNER
January 1991

Première vue from *Douze vues du pays de Salzbourg* (Mannheim, 1807) [The British Library: Map Library - Maps.K.7.Tab.64.(3.)]

THE
SALZBURG
YEARS
1756-1781

Birth and early years

Even without his son, Leopold Mozart (1719–1787) *(1)* would have been guaranteed a place in the history books. He was a gifted musician, and in 1756, the year of Mozart's birth, was a violinist in the private orchestra at the court of the ruling Prince-Archbishop of Salzburg, Siegmund Christoph, Count of Schrattenbach. He had come to Salzburg from his parental home in Augsburg in 1737 to study at the University with the intention of becoming a priest, but his love of music had led him instead to take up an appointment initially with the Canon of Salzburg before joining the Archbishop's household. At the time of Mozart's birth Leopold was working on his *Versuch einer gründlichen Violinschule* [Treatise on the fundamentals of violin-playing], a highly important theoretical and practical treatise, published later that year *(2)*; it remained the standard violin method for a considerable time, both in the original German and in various translations.

An early review of the *Violinschule* gives a contemporary evaluation of Leopold's abilities as a teacher:

1 Leopold Mozart, *Versuch einer gründlichen Violinschule*, (Augsburg, 1756) [The British Library: Music Library – d.2.a., frontis]

A work of this kind has long been wished for . . . Those who are most adept at wielding the bow are not always in control of the pen, and the few who possess equal facility in both often lack the will to write. How much the greater, then, is our obligation towards the author of the present work. The thorough and accomplished virtuoso, the reasonable and methodical teacher, the learned musician — these characteristics . . . are all here revealed in one . . . for many of those, too, who profess the violin will here find instruction, and will do well to profit by this great master's teaching, so as no longer to spoil their pupils with bad precepts.[1]

This 'methodical teacher' was blessed with two musically gifted children — Maria Anna, named after her mother but known as 'Nannerl' (born 30/31 July 1751) — and Wolfgang Amadeus, as he is now known,[2] (born 27 January 1756). Mozart's place in history is due in part to the fact that his father recognised and nurtured his talent from an early age, virtually giving over his life in order to assist in the advancement of his son. Moreover, the fact that we know so much about Mozart's early years is due entirely to Leopold's desire to record the events in his son's life. Early evidence of the musical progress of the two children survives in the form of a small music book *(3)* prepared by Leopold, initially for Nannerl's use, but subsequently used also to indicate the works learnt by the four-year-old Mozart and to record his earliest compositions, K.1a-d.[3] Some are entered in Leopold's hand and some by Mozart.

The Archbishop encouraged the musicians at his court to travel to Italy to study. Support of this kind was to enable Leopold to take his two young children on long musical tours throughout their formative years, tours which exposed them to a variety of European cultures and styles and which were consequently to direct the course of Mozart's development as a musician. Their first trip was to Munich (12 January 1762 for three weeks). Little is known of the visit other than that Mozart appeared before the Bavarian Elector Maximilian III Joseph. Later, on 18 September 1762, the whole family went to Vienna. Details of this visit survive largely in the form of Leopold's letters to his landlord and banker in Salzburg, Johann Lorenz Hagenauer (1712-1792), as well as newspaper reports. They were invited to court to perform for the Empress Maria Theresa and Emperor Francis I.

Their Majesties received us with such extraordinary graciousness that, when I shall tell

2 Leopold Mozart, *Versuch einer gründlichen Violinschule*, (Augsburg, 1756) [The British Library: Music Library – d.2.a., title-page]

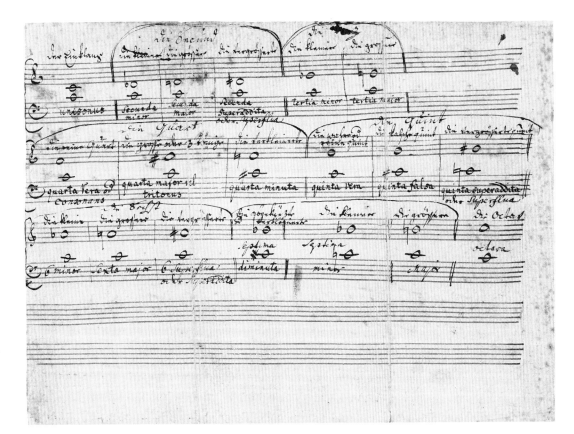

3 Mozart's earliest compositions — K.1a–d. Two leaves extracted from Nannerl's 'Notenbuch'. Both in Leopold's handwriting. First leaf contains diagrams of musical intervals with their Latin and German descriptions. The other side of this leaf contains Mozart's earliest surviving compositions, again in his father's hand. These works date from 1761.

A substantial portion of the 'Notenbuch' survives, though some of the leaves were detached (probably after Mozart's death): two of these came to light in 1954 and are now in The Pierpont Morgan Library. [The Pierpont Morgan Library: Mary Flagler Cary Music Collection]

it, people will declare that I have made it up. Suffice it is to say that Woferl jumped up on the Empress's lap, put his arms round her neck and kissed her heartily. (16 October 1762)

The grand European Tour — to England and back 1763–1766

In June 1763 Leopold was given leave to travel with his family and a coachman to the principal musical centres of Europe. Travel was a hazardous business in the eighteenth century: two days after they set off Leopold wrote:

That was a snail's journey . . . Two hours outside Wasserburg a back wheel broke in pieces and there we were stranded. (11 June 1763)

The family had to wait about two days for the wheel to be fixed (involving expenditure on housing, and feeding the horses and the driver). During the wait Mozart was given the chance of trying an organ in the local church (something he was to do in many of the towns that the family later visited):

I explained to Woferl the use of the pedal. Whereupon he tried it *stante pede*, shoved the stool away and played standing at the organ, at the same time working the pedal, and doing it all as if he had been practising it for several months. Everyone was amazed. Indeed this is a fresh act of God's grace, which many a one only receives after much labour. (11 June 1763)

Their journey took them to Munich, where Mozart and Nannerl played again for Elector Maximilian III Joseph of Bavaria and Clemens, Duke of Bavaria. At Ludwigsburg Leopold suspected that his attempts to gain an audience with Karl Eugen, Duke of Wurtemberg were being thwarted by the intervention of Niccolò Jommelli (court Kapellmeister at Stuttgart) who was attempting to prevent Germans from appearing before the Duke. Even when they were secured, performances at court did not always bring the rewards Leopold hoped for:

If the kisses which she [Princess Amalia at Aachen] gave to my children, and to Wolfgang especially, had been all new louis d'or, we should be quite happy; but neither the innkeeper nor the postmaster are paid in kisses. . . Little Wolfgang has been given two magnificent swords . . . My little girl has received Dutch lace . . . cloaks, coats and so forth. With snuff-boxes and étuis and such stuff we shall soon be able to rig out a stall (17 October 1763)

After stopping at Wasserburg, Munich, Augsburg, Mainz, Frankfurt, Coblenz, Bonn, Cologne, Aachen, Liège, and Brussels the family finally arrived in Paris in November 1763. The city was in mourning for Marie-Thérèse de Bourbon (first wife of the Dauphin Louis) and it was some time before the prospect of playing at court arose. Shortly after their arrival the Mozarts met Friedrich Melchior Grimm, an influential diplomat and secretary to the Duke of Orleans. Grimm was extremely impressed with the two children:

True prodigies are sufficiently rare to be worth speaking of . . . A Kapellmeister of Salzburg, [Leopold had been appointed Vice-Kapellmeister in February 1763] Mozart by name, has just arrived here with two children . . . His daughter, eleven years of age, plays the harpsichord in the most brilliant manner; she performs the longest and most difficult pieces with an astonishing precision. Her brother, who will be seven years old next February, is such an extraordinary phenomenon that one is hard put to believe what one sees with one's eyes and hears with one's ears. It means little for this child to perform with the greatest precision the most difficult pieces, with hands that can hardly stretch a sixth; but what is really incredible is to see him improvise for an hour on end and in doing so give rein to the inspiration of his genius and to a mass of enchanting

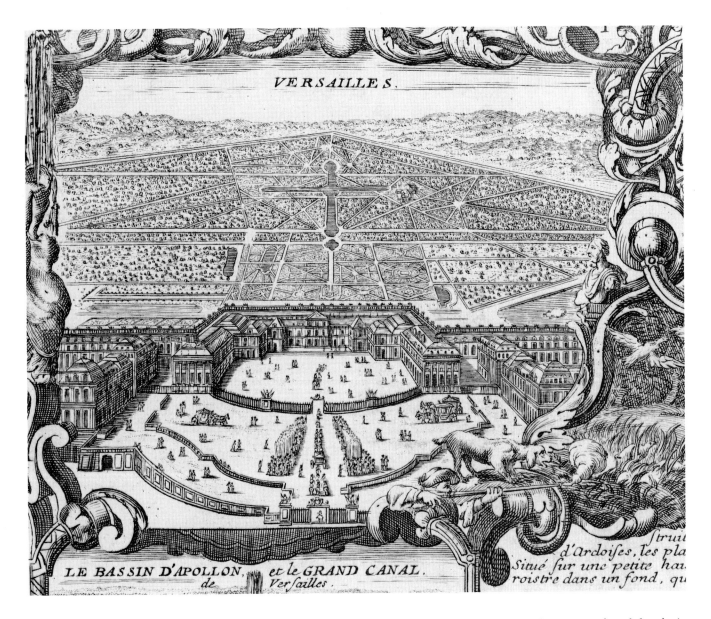

VERSAILLES.

LE BASSIN D'APOLLON, et le GRAND CANAL.
de Versailles.

struit
d'Ardoises, les pla
Situé sur une petite hau.
roistre dans un fond, qu

4 Versailles from *Nouveau Plan de Paris*, 1766. [The British Library: Map Library – Maps.K.64.34.]

ideas ... The most consummate Kapellmeister could not be more profound than he in the science of harmony and of modulations ... He has such great familiarity with the keyboard that when it is hidden for him by a cloth spread over it, he plays on this cloth with the same speed and the same precision. To read at sight whatever is submitted to him is child's play ... he makes me realize that it is difficult to guard against madness on seeing prodigies.[4]

Just before Christmas the family went to Versailles *(4)*, staying there for two weeks. Leopold described the visit to his landlord's wife:

I heard good and bad music there. Everything sung by individual voices and supposed to resemble an aria was empty, frozen and wretched — in a word, French; but the choruses are good and even excellent. So every day I have been with my little man to see the Mass in the Royal Chapel, to hear the choir in the motet, which is always performed there. (1 February 1764)

In the same letter he outlined musical life in Paris:

There is a perpetual war here between the Italian and the French music. The whole of French music is not worth a sou ... The Germans are taking the lead in the publication

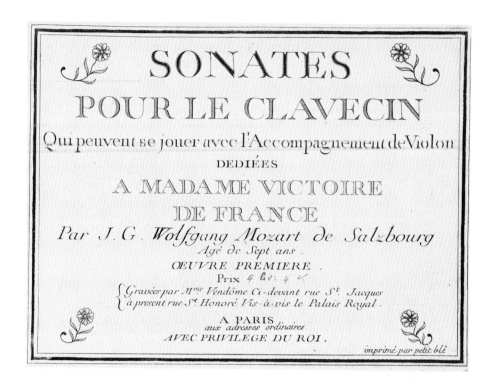

5 Wolfgang Amadeus Mozart *Sonates pour le clavecin* ... (Paris, 1764) K.6&7. Mozart's first works to appear in print. Two sonatas for keyboard and violin in C and D major, These are dedicated to Madame Victoire, second daughter of Louis XV. [The British Library: Music Library – Hirsch IV. 1, title-page]

of their compositions . . . Schobert, Eckardt, Le Grand and Hochbrucker have all brought us their engraved sonatas and presented them to my children. At present four sonatas of M. Wolfgang Mozart are being engraved. Picture to yourself the furore which they will make in the world when people read on the title-page that they have been composed by a seven-year-old child; and when the sceptics are challenged to test him, as he already has been, imagine the sensation when he asks someone to write down a minuet or some tune or other and then immediately and without touching the clavier writes in the bass and, if it is wanted, the second violin part . . . every day God performs fresh miracles through this child. By the time we reach home, God willing, he will be able to contribute to the court music. He frequently accompanies in public concerts. He even, when accompanying, transposes a prima vista; and everywhere Italian or French works are put before him, which he plays off at sight.

The compositions were sonatas for keyboard and violin K.6 and K.7 (published as op.I, *(5)*) and K.8 and K.9 (published as op.II).

In April 1764 the Mozarts left for London, having been urged to do so by their contacts in Paris. Altogether they were to spend 15 months in the English capital and late in April they made the first of three visits (the others were in May and October) to the court of King George III and Queen Charlotte.

On April 27th we were with the King and Queen in the Queen's Palace in St. James's Park . . . The present was only twenty-four guineas, which we received immediately on leaving the King's apartment, but the graciousness with which both His Majesty the King and Her Majesty the Queen received us cannot be described. In short, their easy manner and friendly ways made us forget that they were the King and Queen of England. At all courts up to the present we have been received with extraordinary courtesy. But the welcome which we have been given here exceeds all others. (28 May 1764)

Young Mozart's abilities were continually being tested with demands that he should sight-read, improvise, compose melodies to pre-set bass lines, accompany other performers etc., and this occasion was no exception:

The King placed before him not only works of Wagenseil, but those of [Johann Christian]

Bach, Abel and Handel and he played off everything *prima vista*. . . . Then he accompanied the Queen in an aria which she sang, and also a flautist who played a solo. Finally he took the bass part of some airs of Handel . . . and played the most beautiful melody on it and in such a manner that everyone was amazed. In short, what he knew when we left Salzburg is a mere shadow compared with what he knows now. It exceeds all that one can imagine . . . He has now continually in his head an opera which he wants to produce there [Salzburg] with several young people. (28 May 1764)

After giving a successful benefit concert (they gave several while in the country - (6)), the Mozarts had planned to visit Kent, though unfortunately Leopold fell ill. The family retired to Chelsea, then about two miles outside London:

It has one of the most beautiful views in the world. Wherever I turn my eyes, I only see gardens and in the distance the finest castles . . . (13 September 1764)

Leopold was in fact suffering from a severe cold:

In England there is a kind of native complaint, which is called a 'cold' . . . [which] in the case of people who are not constitutionally sound becomes so dangerous that in many cases it develops into a 'consumption' . . . and the wisest course for such people to adopt is to leave England and cross the sea.

While Leopold recovered the family had to live without income, though it seems likely that Mozart made use of the interlude to compose his first symphonies. These works were referred to by Leopold in a letter of 8 February 1765:

The symphonies in the concert will all be by Wolfgang Mozart. I must copy them myself, unless I want to pay one shilling for each sheet. Copying music is a very profitable business here.

6 *Public Advertiser* (London 9 May 1764). An advertisement for one of the concerts given in London. [The British Library: General Library – Burney collection]

For the Benefit of Sig. GRAZIANI.

HICKFORD's Great Room, in Brewer-Street, Thursday, May 17, will be a Grand Concert of

Vocal and Iustrumental MUSIC.

The Vocal Parts by the Signoras Sartori, Cremonini, and Signor Maziotti. First Violin, and a Concerto, by Sig. Giardini. Concerto and Solo on the Violoncello, by Sig. Graziani. Concerto on the German Flute by Sig. Florio. Concerto on the Harpsichord by Master Mozart, who is a real Prodigy of Nature; he is but Seven Years of Age, plays any thing at first Sight, and composes amazingly well. He has had the Honour of exhibiting before their Majesties greatly to their Satisfaction. The Whole to conclude with a Full Piece. † Tickets, Half a Guinea each, to be had of Sig. Graziani, at the Warwick-street Coffee-house.

7 *God is our refuge* by Wolfgang, written out with the help of his father and presented to the British Museum in June 1765. [The British Library: Music Library – K.10.a.17.(3.)]

Meanwhile Queen Charlotte had asked to be the dedicatee of some of Mozart's works which Leopold duly had engraved at his own expense (K.10–15, sonatas for keyboard and violin or flute and 'cello, published as op.III).

Towards the end of their stay in London the Mozarts visited the British Museum (in its original home in Montagu House on the site of the present building (PLATE II). Nannerl, in an undated entry in her travel diary, relates her visit to 'the library, the antiquities, birds of all kinds, fishes, insects, fruits . . . a rattlesnake'. Children were not normally admitted, so Nannerl and Mozart were privileged. They presented the Museum with copies of the publications of his op.I and op.II sonatas (K.6–9), a copy of J. B. Delafosse's engraving of the watercolour of Leopold and his children by Louis Carrogis de Carmontelle (*see* PLATE I) and the manuscript of Mozart's specially composed four-part vocal composition 'God is our Refuge', K.20, written out with the help of his father *(7)*. This was to remain his only setting of English words. On another visit, it seems, Leopold gave the Museum a copy of Mozart's op.III (K.10–15).[5]

The Mozarts left England in August 1765, travelling by way of Canterbury, to Dover, across the channel to Calais and then to The Hague where they had been invited to perform before Princess Caroline of Nassau-Weilburg. Their journey was severely delayed owing to Leopold, Nannerl and Mozart suffering illnesses. Eventually they reached Paris in May 1766, travelling then through Switzerland and Germany and finally arriving home in Salzburg in late November. Mozart's reputation preceded him on the return trip, and the family were frequently detained so that he could give performances and display his talents. The young boy's skills are summed up in an account published in October 1766:

You will have seen, with as much surprise as pleasure, a child of nine play the harpsichord like the great masters; & what will have astonished you even more was to hear from trustworthy persons that he already played it in a superior manner three years ago; to know that almost everything he plays is of his own composition; to have found in all his pieces, and even in his improvisations, that character of force which is the stamp of genius, that variety which proclaims the fire of imagination & that charm which proves an assured taste; and lastly, to have seen him perform the most difficult pieces with an ease and a facility that would be surprising even in a musician of thirty . . . It may be predicted with confidence that he will one day be one of the greatest masters of his art.[6]

Salzburg 1766

After his return Mozart's compositions included experiments with keyboard concerto writing in the form of arrangements of sonata movements of works by some of the composers he had met on his journeys (Honnauer, Eckard etc) *(8)*. This afforded the opportunity for him both to become familiar with other music, and to come to grips with concerto movement forms unhampered by the need to create the thematic and harmonic material as well. During this period he also wrote the first act of the 'sacred Singspiel' *Die Schuldigkeit des ersten Gebots (9)*, the remaining acts being written by Michael Haydn (1737–1806, then Konzertmeister to the Archbishop of Salzburg) and Anton Adlgasser (1729–1777, court and cathedral organist in Salzburg). The first performance took place on 12 March 1767 as part of the traditional annual performance by the students of the Gymnasium. On one occasion Mozart was locked in a room to compose in order to convince the Archbishop of Salzburg of his abilities as a composer. Duly satisfied, the Archbishop continued in his support of the

8 Cadenza to the first movement of one of Mozart's 'pastiche' keyboard concertos, K.40. [The British Library: Department of Manuscripts – Add. MS 47861A, f.10ʳ]

9 First part of cantata *Die Schuldigkeit des ersten Gebots*, K.35. The secco recitative section for the Spirits of Mercy, Justice and Christ from the second aria of the work. Mozart has shortened the passage, by deleting the end. [Windsor Castle, Royal Library. © Her Majesty Queen Elizabeth II]

family, giving them leave to travel and even advancing them sums of money to help them to do so.

Vienna 1767–1769 — *La finta semplice*

The Mozarts' second visit to Vienna began in September 1767, coinciding with the planned festivities for the marriage of the Archduchess Maria Josepha to King Ferdinand of Naples. Sadly the Archduchess died during a smallpox epidemic before the wedding took place. The period of mourning brought court activities to an end, leaving the Mozarts no chance to perform. These circumstances, along with the health risk, convinced Leopold of the need to leave the city for a while. The family travelled to Brno and to Olomouc, but nevertheless both Mozart and his sister suffered mild attacks of smallpox. It is clear from Leopold's letters to Hagenauer that Mozart had by then written a substantial number of pieces, many of them commissions.

On their return to Vienna they appeared before the Emperor who failed to reward them, and Leopold became convinced that members of the aristocracy were deliberately avoiding Mozart so that they could dismiss his talents as humbug and foolishness; that it was all prearranged; that he was given music which he

already knew; that it was ridiculous to think that he could compose, and so forth. (30 January – 3 February 1768)

Leopold contrived a situation where one of these sceptics, another composer, was to hear Mozart perform a

most extraordinarily difficult concerto ... So we turned up and the fellow had the opportunity, therefore, of hearing his concerto played off by little Wolfgang as if he knew it by heart ... Finally he declared: All I can say as an honest person is that this boy is the greatest man now living in the world. It was impossible to believe it. But in order to convince the public of what it really amounts to, I decided to do something entirely out of the ordinary, that is, to get Wolfgang to write an opera for the theatre. (30 January – 3 February 1768)

Leopold went on to report that the Emperor had in fact suggested that Mozart write an opera:

What do you think? Is not the reputation of having written an opera for the Viennese theatre the best way to enhance one's credit not only in Germany but also in Italy?

The opera was *La finta semplice*, but growing opposition to the project within the musical establishment ultimately prevented it from being performed. In

10 Leopold's Petition about *La Finta Semplice*. This is apparently a draft of the petition sent to Joseph II. [Glasgow University Library, MS Farmer 271/8. By permission of the Librarian]

May, after receiving from the Emperor introductions to the various states in Italy, Leopold wrote to Hagenauer

Or should I perhaps sit down in Salzburg with the empty hope of some better fortune, let Wolfgang grow up, and allow myself and my children to be made fools of until I reach the age which prevents me from travelling and until he attains the age and physical appearance which no longer attract admiration for his merits? Is my child to have taken the first step with this opera for nothing . . . (11 May 1768)

In July he expressed his anger more strongly:

All sensible people must with shame agree that it is a disgrace to our nation that we Germans are trying to suppress a German, to whom foreign countries have done justice by their great admiration and even by public acknowledgments in writing. (30 July 1768)

And in September — over a year after they had left Salzburg — he wrote:

As for Wolfgang's opera all I can tell you is that, to put it shortly, the whole hell of musicians has arisen to prevent the display of a child's ability. I cannot even press for its performance, since a conspiracy has been formed to produce it, if it must be produced, extremely badly and thus ruin it. I have to await the arrival of the Emperor. (14 September)

Mozart père & ses deux enfans.   1777.

PLATE I   Leopold Mozart with his children. Watercolour by Louis Carrogis de Carmontelle [The British Museum: Department of Prints and Drawings – BM 1972 U.653]

PLATE II British Museum courtyard. Watercolour by Wykeham Archer. [The British Museum: Department of Prints and Drawings – 1914-2-6-23]

PLATE III Thomas Linley the Younger. Oil painting by Thomas Gainsborough probably painted *ca*. 1773/4. [Dulwich Picture Gallery: No.331 By permission of the Governors of Dulwich Picture Gallery]

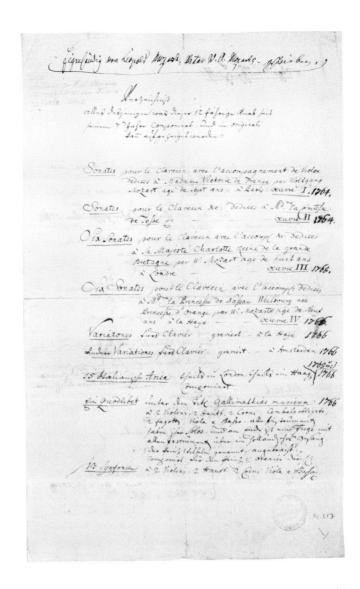

11 Leopold's list of Mozart's works – page 1 which shows earliest publications [Paris, Bibliothèque du Conservatoire, MS 263]

On 28 September Leopold sent a petition *(10)* to Emperor Joseph II detailing the events surrounding the composition and non-performance of the opera:

… A learned paper from Paris has confirmed this opinion by declaring, after an exhaustive description of my son's genius, that there was no doubt that this child would at the age of twelve write an opera for one or the other of the Italian theatres; but everybody thought that a German should reserve such glory for his own country alone. I was unanimously encouraged therein …[7]

He concluded by saying:

I humbly and obediently beg for a close examination of the musical powers of my child, above all for the sake of his honour.

Also about this time Leopold compiled a list entitled 'Verzeichniss alles desjenigen was dieser 12jährige Knab seit seinem 7tem Jahre componiert, und in originali kann aufgezeiget werden' — [List of everything that this 12-year-old boy has composed since his 7th year, and can be exhibited in the originals] *(11)*,[8] and this may be a draft or copy of a document which accompanied the petition to Emperor Joseph II.

Although *La finta semplice* was not performed in Vienna, Mozart's one act German Singspiel *Bastien und Bastienne*, composed the same year, was given a private performance, and on 7 December Mozart both conducted and performed in his own music presented at the consecration of a new church at the Orphanage on the Rennweg in the presence of Empress Maria Theresa.

Salzburg 1769 — honorary appointment at court

The family returned to Salzburg on 5 January 1769, shortly before Mozart's 13th birthday, and finally (on 1 May) heard his opera *La finta semplice* performed in the city. During the summer months various compositions by Mozart were performed at Salzburg, including a Mass and some music for the end of the University term. Meanwhile plans were made for a visit to Italy. The Mozarts were not only granted leave, but on this occasion presented with money by the Prince Archbishop. On 27 November, just before their departure, Mozart was granted the title of Concert Master — an honorary appointment which was to become a paid post on his return from Italy: now he had not only a title, but also a position, in Salzburg.

Three Italian Journeys 1769–1773

FIRST VISIT — 1769–1771

Italy was in many ways at the heart of musical activities during the eighteenth century; composers came from other countries to study at the various centres and Italian music was exported the world over. Leopold probably hoped that if his son won favour in Italy his future would be secure both there and elsewhere.

In all, father and son made three trips there, and details of their experiences were related back to Maria Anna and Nannerl by Leopold, with occasional postscripts by Mozart. The earliest of these postscripts to survive dates from the day after their departure on the first trip *(12)*. Although the highlights of the visits were to be commissions to write for the stage, the bulk of Mozart's time was taken up writing and performing instrumental works for private performances. Leopold realised very early on in the first visit that their money would not be made by giving public performances,

for everybody goes in free . . . in Mantua the nobles, the military class and the eminent citizens may all attend them, because they are subsidised by Her Majesty the Empress. (26 January 1770)

Their schedule during the first visit was a punishing one: they visited Rovereto, Verona, Mantua, Cremona, Milan, Lodi, Bologna, Rome, Florence and Naples in the space of six months. Throughout this time the fourteen-year-old Mozart was writing and performing music, hearing other music performed and seeing the local sights.

In March 1770 Mozart received a commission to write the first opera for the following carnival season in Milan. As the season did not begin until Christmas, this meant that they would be away considerably longer than originally intended, and so permission for additional leave of absence was sought from the Archbishop. Mozart was to send the recitatives to Milan by October, and was instructed to arrive by 1 November to write the remaining music. In June his mother enquired about progress only to be told 'Why, he is not even thinking of it . . . so far we know nothing either about the cast or about the libretto'. (30 June 1770)

Before returning to Milan they travelled first to Bologna and Leopold wrote to his wife:

12 Mozart's earliest surviving letter, a postscript to his father's letter of 14 December 1769. This letter was written the day after father and son set off for Italy. Wolfgang's postscript, to his mother, is in German; another, to his sister, is in Italian. 'My heart is completely enchanted with all these pleasures, because it is so jolly on this journey, because it is so warm in the carriage and because our coachman is a fine fellow who, when the road gives him the slightest chance, drives so fast. Papa will have already described the journey to Mamma. The reason I am writing to Mamma is to show her that I know my duty and that I am with the deepest respect her devoted son.' Earlier letters of Wolfgang survive only in copies. [The Pierpont Morgan Library: Morgan MA 836]

What especially pleases me is that we are extraordinarily popular and that Wolfgang is admired here even more than he has been in all the other towns of Italy; the reason is that Bologna is the centre and dwelling-place of many masters, artists and scholars. Here too he has been most thoroughly tested, and the fact that Padre Martini[9], the idol of the Italians, speaks of him with great admiration and has himself set him all the tests, has increased his reputation all over Italy. We have visited him twice and each time Wolfgang has worked out a fugue . . . (27 March 1770)

Then in Florence they met and befriended a young violinist, Thomas Linley (1756-1778) (PLATE III)

who plays most beautifully and who is the same age and the same size as Wolfgang . . . The two boys performed one after the other throughout the whole evening . . . On the following day the little Englishman . . . had his violin brought to our rooms and played the whole afternoon, Wolfgang accompanying on his own. (21 April 1770)

From Rome Leopold related the now famous story of how his son wrote out Allegri's *Miserere*, having heard it just once in the Sistine Chapel; on 8 July Pope Clement XIV conferred upon Mozart the Order of the Golden Spur. Mozart finally received details of the libretto he was to set, *Mitridate, Re di Ponto* (13),

Al destin che la — minaccia togli' oh

13 Late 18th–century copy of *Mitridate, Rè di ponto*, K.87/74a, showing the florid beginning of Aspasia's first aria 'Al destin, che la minaccia'. The part was originally written for Antonia Bernasconi who had earlier appeared in Vienna in Gluck's *Alceste* in 1767. On 17 November Leopold wrote 'The prima donna is infinitely pleased with her arias'. Apparently on the first night of the opera, contrary to the usual customs, the audience insisted on hearing one of Bernasconi's arias repeated, and many arias were applauded. The management became worried that if the calls for encores were to continue the opera, with its three ballets, lasting six hours, would be so long that the nobility would not be home in time for supper. The solution was to cut the length of the ballets. [The British Library: Department of Manuscripts – Add. MS 16058, f 21ᵛ]

and the names of the singers on 28 July. Returning through Bologna he passed various tests for membership of the Accademia Filarmonica and was awarded a diploma, the conditions of entry, stipulating that members must be over the age of 20, having been waived on this occasion.

Mozart could not begin composing the arias to his opera before reaching Milan because they had to be written to suit each singer's voice. Despite the fact that he was unable to begin the part of Sifare until 1 December when the singer arrived in Milan — only 25 days before the first scheduled performance — the première nevertheless took place, as planned, on 26 December, and the opera received another 21 performances that season. On 15 December Leopold had reported that:

The copyist is absolutely delighted, which is a good omen in Italy, where, if the music is a success, the copyist by selling the arias sometimes makes more money than the Kapellmeister does by his composition.

SECOND VISIT 1771 — COMMISSION FROM THE EMPRESS

The second visit, to Milan, from August to September 1771, was occasioned by a commission from Empress Maria Theresa to compose a work for the marriage of her son, Archduke Ferdinand, to Princess Maria Beatrice Ricciarda of Modena — *Ascanio in Alba*, a dramatic serenata. The text of the work had to be submitted to Vienna for approval and by 24 August it had still not arrived for Mozart to set (the wedding was to take place in October). On arrival in Milan Mozart wryly remarked on his fellow lodgers:

Upstairs we have a violinist, downstairs another one, in the next room a singing-master who gives lessons, and in the other room opposite ours an oboist. That is good fun when you are composing! It gives you plenty of ideas. (24 August 1771)

Mozart wrote several symphonies during the Italian visits, some displaying Italian influences such as first movements with little or no development sections, or linked first and second movements. Others, such as the substantial four-movement symphony in F major, K.112 *(14)*, display German, rather than Italian influence, most obviously in the inclusion of a minuet and trio, which was unusual in Italian symphonies of the period.

Mozart and his father returned to Salzburg in December 1771. By this time Mozart had been commissioned to write the first opera for the carnival in Milan the following year. In February 1772 Leopold wrote to the publisher J. G. I. Breitkopf in Leipzig offering some of his son's compositions for publication.

As my son has again won great honour by his composition of the dramatic serenata, he has been asked to write the first opera for the coming carnival in Milan and immediately afterwards the second opera for the Teatro San Benedetto in Venice [this second commission was never, in fact, carried out]. . . . Should you wish to print any of my son's compositions, this intervening period would be the best time to order them. (7 February 1772)

The interval between the second and third Italian trips coincided with the death of Archbishop Schrattenbach. The interference of the Imperial court in Vienna in the election of the new ruler resulted in the appointment of Hieronymus, Count of Colloredo, Prince-Bishop of Gurk and son of the imperial vice-chancellor. Colloredo, who seems to have been unpopular from the start, set about modernising the archdiocese in line with the reforms being undertaken by Joseph II (Holy Roman Emperor and, with his mother, Maria Theresa, co-regent of the Habsburg Empire since the death of his father, Francis Stephen in 1765). These reforms were ultimately to cause the falling off in the composition of orchestrally accompanied church music as such accompaniments would only be required for special feast days and there would be no place for it in everyday circumstances. Nevertheless, under Colloredo Mozart's honorary appointment as Konzertmeister was confirmed and he was formally appointed to the post with a salary of 150 florins/gulden per annum in August 1772.

THIRD VISIT 1772-1773 — OPERATIC COMMISSION

The trip to Milan was made in order to write the first opera, *Lucio Silla*, for the 1772-1773 carnival season there. Mozart received the libretto in advance and composed some of the recitatives in Salzburg. However the librettist, Giovanni De Gamerra (1743-1803), had also sent the libretto to Pietro Metastasio in Vienna who subsequently made various suggestions for improvement, including the addition of a scene in the second act, so Mozart had to rewrite some of his music. Again Mozart's composition of the arias was delayed through the very late arrival of some of the principal singers:

14 Symphony in F major, K.112, showing the end of the Andante in Mozart's hand and the beginning of the minuet in Leopold's. Composed Milan 2 November 1771. The minuet is thought possibly to have originated as a dance movement (one indication of which is that the violas double the bass line rather than having independent parts as was customary in Mozart's symphonic works). Additionally, the fact that this part of the movement was written out by Leopold suggests that Mozart may have been working on another part of the symphony while his father was copying the part that already existed. [The Pierpont Morgan Library: Dannie and Hettie Heineman Collection]

These blessed theatrical people leave everything to the very last minute. (12 December 1772)

The opera went ahead as planned, though not without some mishaps, recounted by Leopold:

The opera was a great success, although on the first evening several very distressing incidents took place. The first hitch was that the performance . . . started three hours late . . . Thus it did not finish until two o'clock in the morning . . . Picture to yourself the whole theatre which by half past five was so full that not another soul could get in. On the first evening the singers are always very nervous at having to perform before such a distinguished audience. But for three hours singers, orchestra and audience (many of the latter stading) had to wait impatiently in the overheated atmosphere until the opera should begin. Next, the tenor, who was engaged as a stop-gap, is a church singer from Lodi who has never before acted on such a big stage, who has only taken the part of the primo tenore a couple of times, and who moreover was only engaged a week before the performance. At the point where in her first aria the prima donna expected from him an angry gesture, he exaggerated his anger so much that he looked as if he was about

to box her ears and strike her on the nose with his fist. This made the audience laugh. Signora De Amicis, carried along by her own enthusiasm, did not realise why they were laughing, and, being thus taken aback, did not sing well for the rest of the evening. (2 January 1773)

Despite these first-night upsets *Lucio Silla* (15) succeeded to such an extent that the second opera, which was to have begun on 23 January, was put back in order to allow for additional performances (26 in all).

Mozart returned to Salzburg for four months. The four symphonies written during this time reflect Italian influences in their design and content. The E flat major work, K.184/161a, in particular, with its three movements proceeding without a break, much in the manner of an Italian overture, uses, in its slow movement, a sighing figure reminiscent of a tragic Italian aria (16).

Vienna 1773 — in hope of an appointment at court?

In July 1773, following the three highly successful Italian visits, Mozart and his

15 Late 18th–century copy of *Lucio Silla*, K.135. Giunia's aria, 'Parto m'affretto', No.16, sung in the first performance by Anna de Amicis-Buonsollazzi, of whom Leopold wrote: 'De Amacis is our best friend. She sings and acts like an angel and is extremely pleased because Wolfgang has served her extraordinarily well.' (26 December 1772). [The British Library: Department of Manuscripts – Add. MS 16057, f.200ʳ]

16 Symphony in E flat, K.184/161a, showing the opening of the second movement in Mozart's hand; the end of the first movement is in the hand of a copyist. [From The Robert Owen Lehman Collection, on deposit in The Pierpont Morgan Library]

father again travelled to Vienna. The reasons for the visit are not entirely clear and Leopold's letters to his wife do not elaborate on his aims, their success or otherwise, since he was constantly concerned that the Salzburg censors were reading his mail. Plans for the first of the Italian journeys had been hatched in Vienna, and Leopold had obtained letters of recommendation from the Emperor, among others. So with his son's reputation now unequivocally established Leopold may have regarded the time as propitious to secure a position for Mozart at the Viennese court.

On 5 August 1773 Mozart was received by the Empress. Leopold wrote:

Her Majesty the Empress was very gracious to us, but that was all. I am saving up a full account until our return, for it is impossible for me to give it in writing. (12 August 1773)

Later, having been given an extension to his leave by Colloredo, who was himself in Vienna in August, he again wrote:

But there are many matters about which one cannot write . . . We do not know ourselves when we shall leave. It may be soon but there may be some delay. It depends on circumstances which I may not enumerate. (21 August 1773)

During this time Mozart composed a cycle of string quartets, K.168-K.173. It is likely that these works were influenced by Haydn's quartets op.17 and op.20, composed in 1771 and 1772. Like Haydn's works, Mozart's quartets are each in four movements and K.173 has a fugal finale, a device adopted by Haydn in three of his op.20 *(17 & 18)*.

Salzburg 1773–1774

The period immediately following Mozart's return from Vienna in 1773 was marked by the composition of a large number of symphonies. Mozart seems to have begun to refine his style of composition, and two of them at least stand well with the very popular symphonies of the next decade — the Symphony in G Minor, K.183/173dB, written in October 1773 just after his return from Vienna, and the Symphony in A major, K.201/186a, written in April the following year *(see PLATE IV and 19 & 20)*. In 1773 Mozart also wrote his first wholly original piano concerto. The early training, founded on earlier arrangements of pre-existing sonata movements by other composers, was rewarded — the D major Concerto, K.175 remaining a favourite for about ten years. Mozart was often able to report performances of it back to his father.

Smaller works from this period include a Sonata for clavier duet in B flat, K.358/186c, written in the spring of 1774 *(21)*. The keyboard duet had only recently become a viable medium, since the restricted compass of earlier instruments made it difficult to seat two players at one keyboard. Mozart used works of this type both for performance with his sister, and with his pupils.

Munich 1774–1775 — La finta giardiniera

Having been commissioned to write an *opera buffa* for the 1774-75 carnival season in Munich, Mozart, again accompanied by his father, set off in order to complete the composition, *La finta giardiniera*. On this occasion Mozart's sister was to join them later. Once in Munich Leopold set about making arrangements for somewhere for Nannerl to stay. Her journey had already been fixed, as she was to travel with two of their Salzburg friends. Leopold's letters to his wife reveal much about what could be expected on the journey and from them one gains the impression that he did most of the planning for these trips:

17 Draft of the fugal finale for the string quartet in D Minor, K.173. [The British Library: Department of Manuscripts – Zweig 52, f.1ʳ]

18 Quartet in B flat K.172, showing the end of first movement where Mozart has had to cancel one bar and cram the rewritten version onto handwritten staves at the end of the page. Otherwise the score is remarkably clear, indicating that it may possibly be a fair copy. [The British Library: Department of Manuscripts – Add 31749 f.7ʳ]

19 Symphony, K.183/173dB in G minor, opening of first movement. This work has come to be called the 'little g minor', linking it in power and mood to the Symphony in the same key, K.550 of 1788. [From The Robert Owen Lehman Collection, on deposit in The Pierpont Morgan Library]

20 Symphony, K.201/186a in A major, opening of first movement. [From The Robert Owen Lehman Collection, on deposit in The Pierpont Morgan Library]

21 Sonata in B flat for clavier duet,
K.358/186c. Opening of the first
movement. [The British Library:
Department of Manuscripts – Add. MS
14396 f.22ᵛ -23ʳ]

Nannerl must certainly have a fur rug for the journey, or she will not be able to stand
the cold in a half-open coach. She must wrap up her head well and she must protect her
feet with something more than her felt shoes . . . She ought therefore to slip on the fur
boots . . . put a little hay in the bottom of the coach . . . She must try to pack everything
in one box, for she will not need many clothes for twelve days; and she will probably
have to bring a hat-box, though indeed the latter will be a little inconvenient. However,
one advantage is that women's clothes can be folded into a very small space. (21
December 1774)

Unlike the Milan carnival seasons the opera performances in Munich were
attended by a paying audience. So, instead of a long run of one opera followed
by a long run of another, operas would only be performed perhaps twice in
succession and then not again for two or three weeks, during which other
works would be given.

Thus the singers know the parts of at least twenty operas which are performed in turn,
and at the same time they study a new one. (14 December 1774)

Plans for the performance went well, but to do the work justice, the date of the
first performance was delayed,

in order that the singers may learn their parts more thoroughly and thus, knowing the music perfectly, may act with greater confidence and not spoil the opera. To have got it ready by December 29th would have meant a fearful rush. As a musical composition it is indeed amazingly popular, and everything now depends on the stage production . . . (28 December 1774)

The postponement of the opera (it eventually opened on 13 January) meant that Nannerl, who reached Munich on 4 January 1775, was able to hear the first performance. Mozart wrote of its success to his mother:

Thank God! My opera was performed yesterday, the 13th, for the first time and was such a success . . . the whole theatre was so packed that a great many people were turned away . . . After the opera was over and during the pause when there is usually silence until the ballet begins, people kept on clapping all the time and shouting 'Bravo'; now stopping, now beginning again and so on . . . I fear that we cannot return to Salzburg very soon and mamma must not wish it, for she knows how much good it is doing me to be able to breathe freely. We shall come home soon enough. One very urgent and necessary reason for our absence is that next Friday my opera is being performed again and it is most essential that I should be present. Otherwise my work would be quite unrecognizable — for very strange things happen here. (14 January 1775)

This letter gives us an indication that Mozart felt stifled by life in Salzburg, particularly in the employ of Archbishop Colloredo. The Archbishiop arrived in Munich between performances of *La finta giardiniera*, and although he was not to hear the work himself, he learnt about it from the Elector and his family:

Picture to yourself the embarrassment of His Grace the Archbishop at hearing the opera praised by the whole family of the Elector and by all the nobles, and at receiving the enthusiastic congratulations which they all expressed to him. Why, he was so embarrassed. (18 January 1775)

The Mozarts eventually left Munich and arrived back in Salzburg on 7 March 1775, Mozart's opera having been performed only three times (the last of which had had to be cut as the *seconda donna* was ill).

Salzburg 1775–1777 — dissatisfaction with Colloredo

The period after the return from Munich was one of remarkable creativity during which Mozart composed a number of keyboard and violin concertos, the dramatic work *Il Rè pastore*, concert arias, serenades, divertimenti, masses, the *Litaniae de venerabili altaris sacramento*, and chamber works. One of the keyboard concertos, K.246 in C major, was for the 26-year-old Countess Antonia Lützow who, judging by the intricacy of the work, must have been a talented performer. Mozart later took the work with him to Mannheim and Paris, using it as a teaching piece. Three sets of cadenzas survive, the first for the Countess, another for Mozart's own use *(22)*, and a third written after his move to Vienna in the 1780s. Despite all this creative activity Mozart composed no original symphonies until his trip to Paris in 1778. The only symphonies from this period are based on already existing works - *La finta giardiniera*, to which a finale was added, a multi-movement serenade written for the end of the summer university term in Salzburg in 1777, and the overture to the Serenata *Il Rè pastore* again to which a finale was added.

These years in Salzburg were also marked by Mozart's increasing frustration with life under Colloredo. Leopold had evidently requested leave of absence to travel again with his son on at least one occasion, and finally in August 1777 Mozart wrote to the Archbishop:

I will not presume to trouble Your Grace with a full description of our unhappy circumstances, which my father has set forth most accurately in his very humble petition . . . Later my father again applied for leave of absence, which Your Grace refused to grant, though you permitted me, who am in any case only a half-time servant, to travel alone. Our situation is pressing and my father has therefore decided to let me go alone. My conscience tells me that I owe it to God to be grateful to my father, who has spent his time unwearyingly upon my education, so that I may lighten his burden, look after myself and later on be able to support my sister . . . Your Grace will therefore be so good as to allow me to ask you most humbly for my discharge . . . seeing that when I asked you for permission to travel to Vienna three years ago you graciously declared that I had nothing to hope for in Salzburg and would do better to seek my fortune elsewhere. (1 August 1777)

The Archbishop's response was to release both Mozart and his father. However Leopold remained.

Second grand European Tour 1777–1779

Having extricated himself from the Archbishop's service Mozart, this time accompanied by his mother, set off in search of an appointment elsewhere.

22 Cadenzas for the first and second movements of the C major keyboard concerto, K.246 1b & 2b. [The British Library: Department of Manuscripts – Add. MS 61905 f.1ʳ]

Leopold and Nannerl were clearly quite distraught at being parted from Mozart and his mother: '. . .that sad day which I never thought I should have to face. . .' wrote Leopold (25 September 1777). This was the first time that father and son had been separated and it is apparent that Leopold undertook much of the organisation for the visit, advising Mozart and his mother of places to stay, even giving the costs of meals as they made their way through the German states. He also urged his son to secure letters of introduction at all stages.

In Munich Mozart established contact with acquaintances and began to try to secure an audience with the Elector, Maximilian III Joseph. Mozart met Count Seeau who advised him to seek an audience with the Elector at once, and, if that were not possible, to write to him. Even at this early stage in the visit Mozart's relief at being away from Salzburg is apparent:

I am always in my very best spirits, for my heart has been as light as a feather ever since I got away from all that humbug; and, what is more, I have become fatter. (26 September 1777)

In his first letter to his father Mozart referred to Colloredo as 'an idiot', a remark which was not looked upon favourably by Leopold since he was constantly concerned that his letters were being opened and read before he received them.

Mozart's hopes were set back at an early stage for on 29 September he reported a conversation with Prince Zeill who said the Elector had told him:

It is too early yet. He [Mozart] ought to go off, travel to Italy and make a name for himself. I am not refusing him, but it is too soon. (29-30 September 1777)

This comment clearly exasperated Mozart:

Most of these great lords are downright infatuated with Italy. (29-30 September 1777)

Having decided that he would like to remain in Munich Mozart reported a plan to Leopold which he thought might enable him to do so. The scheme involved ten patrons paying one ducat a month (roughly 600 gulden per year). Mozart also hoped that Count Seeau would be prepared to pay him 200 gulden per year.

Now what does Papa think of this idea? . . . For if we have to live in Salzburg on 504 gulden, surely we could manage in Munich on 600 or 800. (29-30 September 1777)[10]

On 30 September Mozart finally had a chance to speak with the Elector, only to be told that there was no vacancy at court. But he remained convinced that if only the Elector could hear him he would change his mind:

As it is he knows nothing whatever about me. He has no idea what I can do . . . I am willing to submit to a test. Let him get together all the composers in Munich, let him even summon a few from Italy, France, Germany, England and Spain. I undertake to compete with any of them in composition. (2 October 1777)

Realising that his son had little chance of success in Munich Leopold began trying to encourage him to lay other plans and Nannerl joined in the plea saying:

It would not do you any credit to stay on in Munich without an appointment. It would do us far more honour if you could succeed in obtaining a post under some other great lord. You will surely find one. (5/6 October 1777)

Nannerl also asked Mozart for

a short preambulum . . . so that I may gradually learn it by heart. (29 September 1777)

Mozart duly obliged and on 11 October wrote to his father:

I enclose four praeambula (23) for her. She will see and hear for herself into what keys they lead.

Mozart was anxious to receive another commission to write an opera; he knew that there was a possibility that he might be asked to write one of the operas for the Naples carnival season, but as yet had had no confirmation.

I have an inexpressible longing to write another opera . . . and once I have composed for Naples I shall be in demand everywhere . . . I am happier when I have something to compose, for that, after all is my sole delight and passion . . . For I have only to hear an opera discussed, I have only to sit in a theatre, hear the orchestra tuning their instruments — oh, I am quite beside myself at once. (11 October 1777)

The travellers proceeded to Augsburg, Leopold's home town, and it was on this visit that Mozart met his cousin, Maria Anna Thekla Mozart, two years his junior. They became friends and under the nick-name 'Bäsle' she later received some of Mozart's most notorious letters (24). While there Mozart attempted to arrange a concert, though his plans were delayed by one week. Meanwhile instructions continued to flow from Salzburg:

You should try to find a copyist . . . wherever you stay for any length of time. For you must really endeavour to get ahead with your composition, and that you can do if you have in readiness copies of symphonies and divertimenti to present to a Prince or to some other patron . . . the divertimenti can be copied very quickly, even though it is true that yours have a number of parts and are rather long . . . For you must not lose sight of

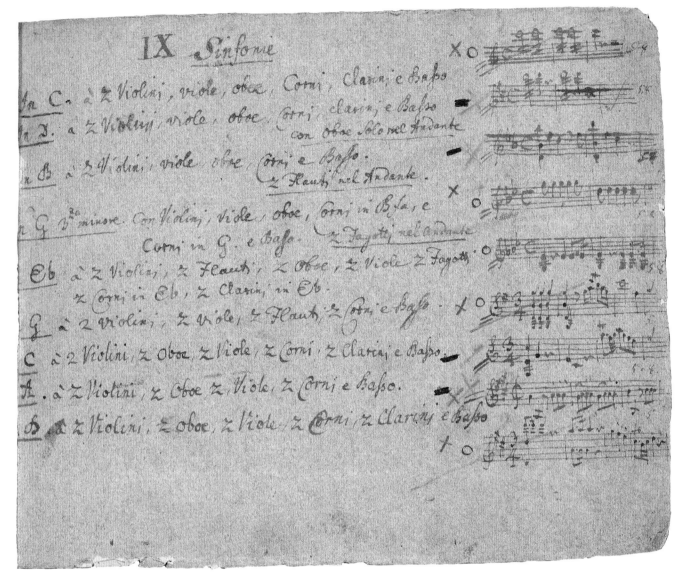

PLATE IV   Leopold's contents page to a volume containing nine of Mozart's Salzburg symphonies composed between 1773 and 1774. The list gives the key of each of the symphonies, the orchestration and a musical incipit for each work. In addition to the G minor and A major symphony, the volume contained Symphonies in E flat major, K.184/161a, G major, K.199/161b, C major, K.162, and D major, K.181/162b composed before Mozart's visit to Vienna, and Symphonies in B flat major, K.182/173dA, C major, K.200/189k and D major, K.202/186b. [From The Robert Owen Lehman Collection, on deposit in The Pierpont Morgan Library]

PLATE V Gavotte for orchestra, K.300. [The Pierpont Morgan Library: Koch 139, f.1ʳ]

23 Two of the four preludes, K.284a = K.396/300g ('praeambula') written for Nannerl, which, until recently, were thought not to have survived. [The Pierpont Morgan Library: Mary Flagler Cary Music Collection]

your main object, which is to make money. All your endeavours should thus be directed to earning money, and you should be very careful to spend as little as possible, or you will not be able to travel in an honourable fashion . . . (15 October 1777)

Mozart took the opportunity of trying out one of the new pianofortes by the Augsburg maker Johann Andreas Stein. Until this visit he had preferred the instruments of Franz Jakob Späth, but he now acknowledged the superiority of the Stein instruments saying that the escapement action meant that the damping of the keys was so much cleaner. The cost of one of Stein's instruments was 300 gulden, twice the annual salary Mozart had been paid in the service of Colloredo. Finally Mozart was able to report to his father that he had given a concert, and that his takings, before expenses, were 90 gulden. After expenses, and having paid off some debts, Mozart and his mother were 26/27 gulden out of pocket which Mozart felt was 'not too bad' (25 October 1777).

The Mozarts then set off for Mannheim, which, under the music-loving Elector Carl Theodor, had one of the finest orchestras in Europe; and since 1742 the Electoral palace had also included an opera house in the west wing. Mozart had every reason to suspect that he would be able to gain some sort of appointment there. Leopold, however, doubted the likelihood of success:

I very much doubt whether Wolfgang will find there all those things which he has

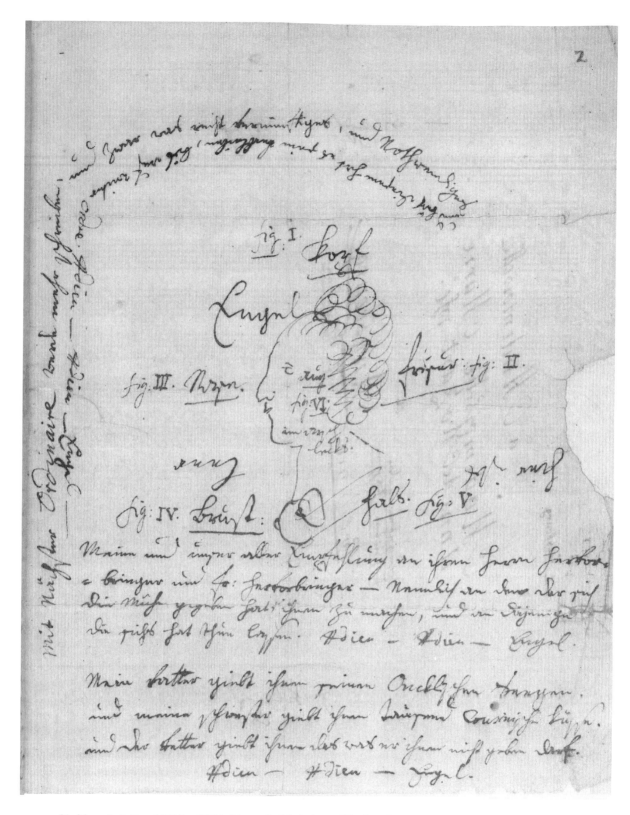

24 Mozart's Letter of 10 May 1779 to his cousin, Maria Anna. [The British Library: Department of Manuscripts – Zweig 67]

imagined and the great advantages which several people may perhaps have described to him. That long journey from Augsburg to Mannheim will have made heavy inroads on your purse and Mannheim will hardly fill it again. (6 November 1777)

Mozart soon met, and became friends with, the violinist Christian Cannabich, director of instrumental music in Mannheim. After waiting around for some considerable time to see if there was any chance that Elector Carl Theodor would offer him even a temporary appointment, Mozart was informed that it was not to be. He eventually managed to secure some work in the form of a commission from a surgeon with the Dutch East India Company at Mannheim, an amateur flautist, to compose 'three short, simple concertos and a couple of quartets for the flute' (10 December 1777), for which he was to be paid 200 gulden. In addition he and his mother were able to obtain free lodgings at the house of the Privy Court Councillor, Serrarius, in return for lessons for his 15-year old daughter.

We can't get up before eight o'clock, for until half past eight there is no daylight in our room . . . I dress in haste and at ten I sit down to compose until about twelve or half past twelve. Then I go to Wendling's, where I again compose a little until half past one, when we have lunch. Thus the time passes until three, when I go . . . to a Dutch officer to give him a lesson in galanterie and thoroughbass, for which I receive . . . four ducats for twelve lessons. At four I must be home again to instruct the daughter of the house . . . At six I go to Cannabich's and give Mlle Rosa her lesson. I stay there to supper, after which we talk or occasionally someone plays. (20 December 1777)

So instead of moving on to Paris before the winter set in, the Mozarts remained in Mannheim. Leopold, meanwhile, became frustrated that his wife and son were taking their journeys lightly:

The object of your journey, the very necessary object was and is and must be, to obtain an appointment or to make money. So far I see little prospect of one or the other. (27 November 1777)

Among his complaints were that Mozart and his mother had stayed too long in Munich and Augsburg using up their money on lodging expenses without having any means of earning money, that Mozart was not keeping him fully apprised of exactly where his plans lay, how he was proposing to get from one place to another and by which route and when, that he was not keeping up with his composition, nor arranging to have existing works copied so that he could present them to an influential Prince or noble, and that he had not taken the right sorts of composition with him — too many symphonies and not enough church music.

Mozart finally made plans to travel to Paris in the spring with Johann Baptist Wendling, a flautist at the Mannheim court orchestra, and the oboist Friedrich Ramm, but nevertheless Leopold's letters show him becoming increasingly exasperated, above all at being in debt as a result of his son's activities. He informed Mozart of his debt on more than one occasion — over 400 gulden on 20 November and 'more than 600 gulden' by 11 December. In February the following year he wrote:

I am now in very deep waters. As you know, I am now in debt to the extent of about 700 gulden and haven't the faintest idea how I am going to support myself, Mamma and your sister on my monthly salary . . . this is the first time I have got into debt. (5 February 1778)

Meanwhile the court organist at Salzburg, Adlgasser, had died suddenly in December 1777 and it was suggested to Leopold that Mozart's name might be put foward for the post. At the same time the Elector Maximilian III of Bavaria was gravely ill. 'The Elector is dying of smallpox . . . This is bound to upset things a bit' wrote Mozart lightheartedly to his father on 27 December 1777. In fact Mozart did not fully appreciate the gravity of the situation. Maximilian had no heirs; on his death Carl Theodor of Mannheim became lawful heir to the Bavarian states and his claim to this position was to result in the War of the Bavarian Succession. More immediately though, Carl Theodor moved to Munich, where members of his court were eventually to follow him, and Mannheim was plunged into a state of mourning with all concert, theatre and opera performances cancelled, and a considerable impact on the local economy.

Mozart, with plans made for his departure to Paris and his mother's return to Salzburg, became attached to a young singer, Aloysia Weber, daughter of Fridolin Weber, a violinist, singer and copyist at the Mannheim court. Declaring that he had actually never really trusted Wendling anyway, Mozart resolved that he would accompany Aloysia to Italy where they would both make their fortune, before going on to Paris. This was the last straw as far as Leopold was concerned:

You are fully acquainted with our difficulties in Salzburg — you know my wretched income, why I kept my promise to let you go away, and all my various troubles. The purpose of your journey was twofold — either to get a good permanent appointment, or, if this should fail, to go off to some big city where large sums of money can be earned. Both plans were designed to assist your parents and to help on your dear sister, but above all to build up your own name and reputation in the world. The latter was partly accomplished in your childhood and boyhood; and it now depends on you alone to raise yourself gradually to a position of eminence, such as no musician has ever obtained. You owe that to the extraordinary talents which you have received from a beneficent God; and now it depends solely on your good sense and your way of life whether you die as an ordinary musician, utterly forgotten by the world, or as a famous Kapellmeister, of whom posterity will read . . . Off with you to Paris! (11-12 February 1778)

As if to add insult to injury, Leopold received Mozart's letter telling him that he had not yet finished his commissions for the Dutchman:

It is not surprising that I have not been able to finish them, for I never have a single quiet hour here. I can only compose at night, so that I can't get up early as well; besides, one is not always in the mood for working. I could, to be sure, scribble off things the whole day long, but a composition of this kind goes out into the world, and naturally I do not want to have cause to be ashamed of my name on the title-page. Moreover, you know that I become quite powerless whenever I am obliged to write for an instrument which I cannot bear [the flute]. Hence as a diversion I compose something else, such as duets for clavier and violin. (14 February 1778)

Paris 1778 — tragedy

On his father's instruction Mozart and his mother set off for Paris in March 1778. Leopold anticipated their arrival there by sending a letter to their former contact, Baron Grimm, explaining the circumstances surrounding Mozart's departure from the Salzburg court and asking that the Baron assist Mozart in any way appropriate on his arrival in Paris. Additionally Mozart's Mannheim friends, Wendling and Ramm, had spread the news of his impending visit and his mother wrote of this to her husband:

Words fail me to tell you how famous and popular is our Wolfgang. Long before we arrived, Herr Wendling had made a great reputation for him and has now introduced him to all his friends. (5 April 1778)

Their prospects looked promising. Mozart was immediately engaged to write some additional choruses for a *Miserere* by the Mannheim Kapellmeister, Ignaz Holzbauer, for performance at the Concert Spirituel,[11] because:

. . . the choruses at Mannheim are weak and poor, whereas in Paris they are powerful and excellent, the choruses he [Holzbauer] has composed would not be effective. (5 April 1778)

Mozart evidently did not find this type of work rewarding:

I may say that I am very glad to have finished that hack-work. (5 April 1778)

He also informed his father that he was to compose a two-act opera entitled *Alexandre et Roxane* as well as a *sinfonia concertante* for his Mannheim friends. His father, in return, continued to offer advice on ways of earning some money:

Do some work occasionally for the theatre, the Concert Spirituel and the Concert des Amateurs, and now and then have something engraved par souscription. (6 April 1778)

On how to go about writing his opera:

I implore you, before you write for the French stage, to listen to their operas and find out what above all pleases them. Well, you will now become a thorough Frenchman and you will endeavour, I hope, to acquire the correct accent. (20 April 1778)

And about getting works published:

If you compose something which is to be engraved, make it easy, suitable for amateurs and rather popular. Don't write in a hurry! Strike out what doesn't satisfy you. Don't do anything gratis; be sure and get paid for everything. (6 May 1778)

Plans for the opera continued for some time:

I must write a grand opera or none at all; if I write a small one, I shall get very little for it (for everything is taxed here). And should it have the misfortune not to please these stupid Frenchmen, all would be over — I should never get another commission to compose . . . the devil himself must certainly have invented the language of these people — and I fully realize the difficulties with which all composers have had to contend. But in spite of this I feel I am as well able to overcome them as anyone else. (31 July 1778)

Later, at the beginning of September, Mozart again outlined risks of composing operas in Paris:

When the opera is finished, it is rehearsed and if these stupid Frenchmen do not like it, it is not performed — and the composer has had all his trouble for nothing. If they think it is good, it is produced and paid for in proportion to its success with the public. There is no certainty whatever. (11 September 1778)

In the event the opera came to nothing, although Mozart did write some of the music for a ballet entitled *Les Petits Riens*. Ballets were often performed as separate entertainments during an operatic evening. *Les Petits Riens* survives only in a copyist's score, making the identification of Mozart's contribution problematic. However, what is thought to have been a discarded movement, a Gavotte in B flat major, K.300, survives in autograph (PLATE V). In addition to this and other commissions, Mozart also took some pupils, including the daughter of the Count of Guines, to whom he was attempting to teach composition.

She has no ideas whatever — nothing comes. I have tried her in every possible way. Among other things I hit on the idea of writing down a very simple minuet, in order to see whether she could not compose a variation on it. It was useless. 'Well', I thought, 'she probably does not know how she ought to begin.' So I started to write a variation on the first bar and told her to go on in the same way and to keep to the idea. In the end it went fairly well. (14 May 1778)

In the same letter Mozart informed his father that he had unofficially been offered the post of organist at Versailles which, if he were to accept, would mean spending six months of the year in Versailles and the remaining six months wherever he liked. He was reluctant to take the post for two reasons: he felt that the salary was not high enough, and he did not like the idea of being confined to one place even for six months of the year. Leopold's response was to urge Mozart not to dismiss the idea so lightly given that the appointment, though not the grandest in itself, might ultimately lead to one of the posts of Kapellmeister there. Leopold continued to keep Mozart and his mother apprised of all that was going on in Salzburg, including accounts of performances of Mozart's compositions. He indicated that he still hoped that Mozart would be offered the post of organist there and hinted at some of the intrigue surrounding the appointment. The salary would be small and there was little hope that the person appointed would be able to supplement the income with teaching:

for there are very few pupils to be had. I have most of them already and besides I enjoy the reputation of being the best teacher. (29 June 1778)

Unknown to Leopold, his son now faced one of the most serious crises of his life: Maria Anna had become dangerously ill and, after a fortnight, died on 3 July. Mozart, knowing that his father would be devastated by the news, sought to prepare him as gently as possible for it by writing to him that she was gravely ill and at the same time writing to their close friend, Bullinger, telling him the whole story, in the hope that Bullinger could support and comfort his father and sister when he finally broke the news to them, which he was intending to do in a second letter to his father. To his father he wrote:

I have very sad and distressing news to give you . . . My dear mother is very ill . . . They give me hope — but I have not much. I have resigned myself wholly to the will of God — and trust that you and my dear sister will do the same . . . for He does nothing without a cause. (3 July 1778)

And to Bullinger:

Mourn with me, my friend! This has been the saddest day of my life . . . I have to tell you that my mother, my dear mother, is no more! God has called her to Himself . . . Only think of all my anxiety, the fears and sorrows I have had to endure for the last fortnight . . . All I ask of you at present is to act the part of a true friend, by preparing my poor father very gently for this sad news . . . May God give him strength and courage! . . . Go to them both at once, I implore you . . . (3 July 1778)

Leopold's response is preserved, since he wrote a letter in three stages. The first wished his wife happiness on her approaching name-day:

Would you have thought a year ago that you would be spending your next name-day in Paris?

He continued on 13 July having received his son's initial letter:

You can imagine what we are both feeling like . . . My dear son! Though I am resigning myself as far as possible to the will of God, you will surely find it quite human and natural that my tears almost prevent me from writing . . . I have complete confidence in your filial love, and know that you have taken all possible care of your devoted mother . . . But if all our hopes are in vain! If we have lost her!

Later that afternoon, after he had talked with Bullinger, he continued:

Bullinger stayed with me, and asked me quietly whether I thought that there was any hope for her . . . I replied that I was convinced not only that she was now dead but that she had died on the day you wrote to me . . . Whereupon he said: 'Yes, she is dead' . . . It is mysteriously sad when death severs a very happy marriage — you have to experience it before you can realize it . . . Great God! To think that I shall have to go to Paris to see her grave! (13 July 1778)

It is perhaps not coincidental that this period of turmoil was to result in a work described as a 'landmark in Mozart's earlier keyboard works, only paralleled in pathos and intensity by the Fantasy and Sonata in C minor'[12] (K.457 and K.475). The Sonata in A minor K.310/300d *(25)* was written in the summer of 1778, following his mother's death and at a time when he was parted from Aloysia Weber.

Any hopes of good prospects in Paris were diminishing and Leopold was anxious that his son should return to Salzburg. The appointment of court organist there was finally offered to Mozart, with the indication that he might one day become Kapellmeister. Leopold related the news, and the Archbishop's excuse for not having allowed father and son to travel the previous year: 'he said that he could not tolerate people going about the world begging' (31 August 1778). Meanwhile the Elector Carl Theodor had taken up residence in Munich, and had invited the members of his court to join him there (though they could stay on at Mannheim and retain their salaries if they wished). Leopold had already written to Padre Martini urging him to send a letter of recommendation to the Elector and, since Munich was on Mozart's route from Paris to Salzburg, he suggested that his son intimate to the Elector, or to a close associate, that he had been offered a post at Salzburg with a salary of 700 or 800 gulden (the actual salary was only 450) in the hope that a more rewarding appointment might be offered. He also told his son that the only reason that he had remained in Salzburg was to ensure that his wife had a pension after his death:

Well, that is all over now, the pension is no longer needed, and so we shall not stand any tyranny but be up and away. (3 September 1778)

Mozart made it quite clear to his father that the only reason he was returning to Salzburg was to be with him:

There is one place where I can say I am at home, where I can live in peace and quiet with my most beloved father and my dearest sister, where I can do as I like, where apart from the duties of my appointment I am my own master, and where I have a permanent income and yet can go off when I like, and travel every second year . . . For I assure you that people who do not travel (I mean those who cultivate the arts and learning) are indeed miserable creatures; and I protest that unless the Archbishop allows me to travel every second year, I can't possibly accept the engagement. A fellow of mediocre talent will remain a mediocrity, whether he travels or not; but one of superior talent (which without impiety I cannot deny that I possess) will go to seed, if he always remains in the same place. If the Archbishop would only trust me, I should soon make his orchestra famous. (11 September 1778)

The sequence of events following Mozart's hurried departure from Paris on 26 September 1778 nearly drove Leopold to distraction. The journey, arranged and paid for by Baron Grimm, was by the slowest means necessitating lengthy stops, where Mozart had to pay living expenses. He decided to abandon this mode of travel. Taking the opportunity of arranging three subscription concerts in Strasburg he got stranded there because of serious flooding. Against all his father's advice and pleading he then proceeded to Mannheim. By this time Leopold was practically beside himself with anger:

25 Sonata for piano, K.310 in A minor, opening showing the end of the first movement and the beginning of the Andante. [From The Robert Owen Lehman Collection, on deposit in The Pierpont Morgan Library]

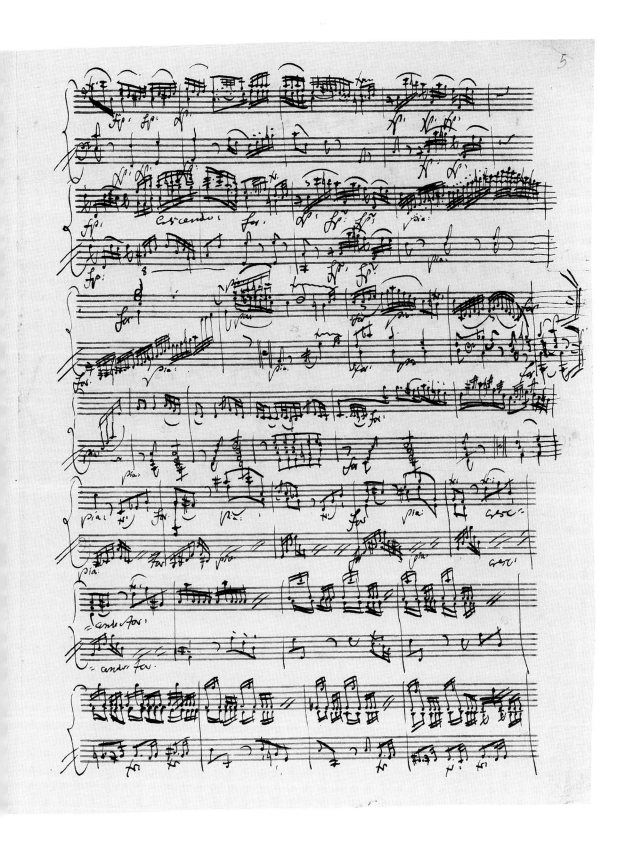

Really, I don't know what to say to you. I shall go mad or die of a decline. The very recollection of all the projects which since your departure from Salzburg you have formed and communicated to me is enough to drive me crazy . . . I could not possibly entertain the mad supposition that you would stay at Mannheim, where there is no longer a court . . . Your whole intention seems to be to ruin me, simply in order to go on building your castles in the air. (19 November 1778)

In this letter Leopold gave exact details of their financial position finishing with the news that Mozart had 'plunged' him into debt to the extent of 863 gulden (Leopold's salary at the time was little over 500 gulden). On 23 November Leopold tried another tack, using his knowledge of his son's love for Aloysia Weber, who had gone to Munich with the court:

By entering the Archbishop's service you will have the advantage of being nearer Munich, which you can reach in eighteen hours, where we can hear about everything . . . and whence Herr Weber and his daughter can visit us and even stay with us.

This letter had the desired effect. Mozart wrote:

I have received your last letter of November 23rd. I am setting off next Wednesday . . . Ah, if only we had clarinets too! You cannot imagine the glorious effect of a symphony with flutes, oboes and clarinets. I shall have much that is new to tell the Archbishop at my first audience and I shall make some suggestions as well. Ah, how much finer and better our orchestra might be, if only the Archbishop desired it. Probably the chief reason why it is not better is because there are far too many performances. (3 December 1778)

Having fully expected his son to return without making any additional stops, Leopold was again let down. With the impending publication of his Violin Sonatas (K.301-K.306 — his first mature works to be printed) which were dedicated to the Electress, Mozart was keen to stop at Munich in order to present them to her himself. Leopold's fear, on the other hand, was that Mozart might lose the appointment in Salzburg and with it the chance to begin paying off the debts. Mozart then wrote asking if he could bring his cousin, Maria Thekla, with him (she has joined him in Munich) but realising that this would necessitate another delay whilst the 'Bäsle' waited for permission from her father in Augsburg, Leopold insisted that his son travel on ahead, and that his niece should follow. Mozart arrived back in Salzburg in mid-January and his certificate of appointment was finally signed on the 17th of that month. During the next twenty months Mozart composed a substantial amount of music, including three symphonies and what was to be his last complete mass setting, K.337 (an incomplete one survives, K.427/417a from 1782, and the Requiem was unfinished at the time of his death).

Munich 1780 — a major operatic commission — Idomeneo

In 1780 Mozart at last received a commission to write an *opera seria* for the carnival in Munich. His knowledge of some of the singers, from previous visits to Munich and Mannheim, enabled him to commence work on the opera whilst still in Salzburg. He left the city on 5 November, little knowing that he would return again only as a visitor.

The libretto for the opera, *Idomeneo*, was based on a French text by Antoine Danchet which had been performed in Paris in 1712 with music by André Campra. Mozart asked Abbate Varesco, Court Chaplain in Salzburg, to provide an Italian text for him. This was not quite ready when Mozart set off for Munich and so Mozart's letters to his father, who acted as intermediary between him and the librettist, reveal a great deal of the process of writing. Not only was the libretto itself being written in Salzburg, but a translation into German was also undertaken there. Mozart, sometimes for dramatic reasons, sometimes at the request of the designer, Lorenzo Quaglio, or one of the singers, frequently asked for alterations to be made in the text which were often strongly resisted by the librettist. Fatherly advice on the composition was offered:

I advise you when composing to consider not only the musical, but also the unmusical public. You must remember that to every ten real connoisseurs there are a hundred ignoramuses. So do not neglect the so-called popular style, which tickles long ears. (11 December 1780)

One of Mozart's worries was the castrato who was to sing the part of Idamante:

When the castrato comes, I have to sing with him, for I have to teach him his whole part as if he were a child. He has not got a farthing's worth of method. (22 November 1780)

The tenor, Anton Raaff, who was singing the title role, caused difficulties for different reasons - he was 65 at the time and his voice was past its best:

Well — the man is old and can no longer show off in such an aria as that in Act II — 'Fuor del mar ho un mar nel seno'. (15 November 1780)

Meanwhile, Leopold continued to convey Varesco's alterations to the text, so that his son could enter them in his own copy which he was using while writing the music. He also questioned some of the proposed cuts:

In this way the recitative will be shortened by a minute, yes, in puncto, by a whole minute. Great gain, forsooth! . . . The question is whether it is worth while to make an alteration by which you will gain at most two and a half minutes . . . It is true that at a rehearsal where the eye has nothing to engage it, a recitative immediately becomes boring; but at the performance, where between the stage and the audience there are so many objects to entertain the eye, a recitative like this is over before the listeners are aware of it. (22 December 1780)

Despite these worries, the rehearsals went well and reports of them reached Salzburg, much to the delight of Leopold:

I have no doubt whatever . . . provided the production is good, I mean provided there are good people to perform it — and that is the case in Munich . . . but when your music is performed by a mediocre orchestra, it will always be the loser, because it is composed with so much discernment for the various instruments and is far from being common-place, as, on the whole, Italian music is. (4 December 1780)

The death of Empress Maria Theresa on 29 November could have meant the cancellation of the opera. However Mozart was able to allay his father's fears:

The death of the Empress does not affect my opera in the least, for none of the theatres have been closed and plays are being performed as usual.

Mozart's father and sister travelled to Munich early in 1781 in order to hear the first performance of the opera on 29 January. In all it received three performances, though because father and son were together at the time their own account of its success was not preserved. On 12 March Mozart left Munich for Vienna, having been summoned there by Colloredo.

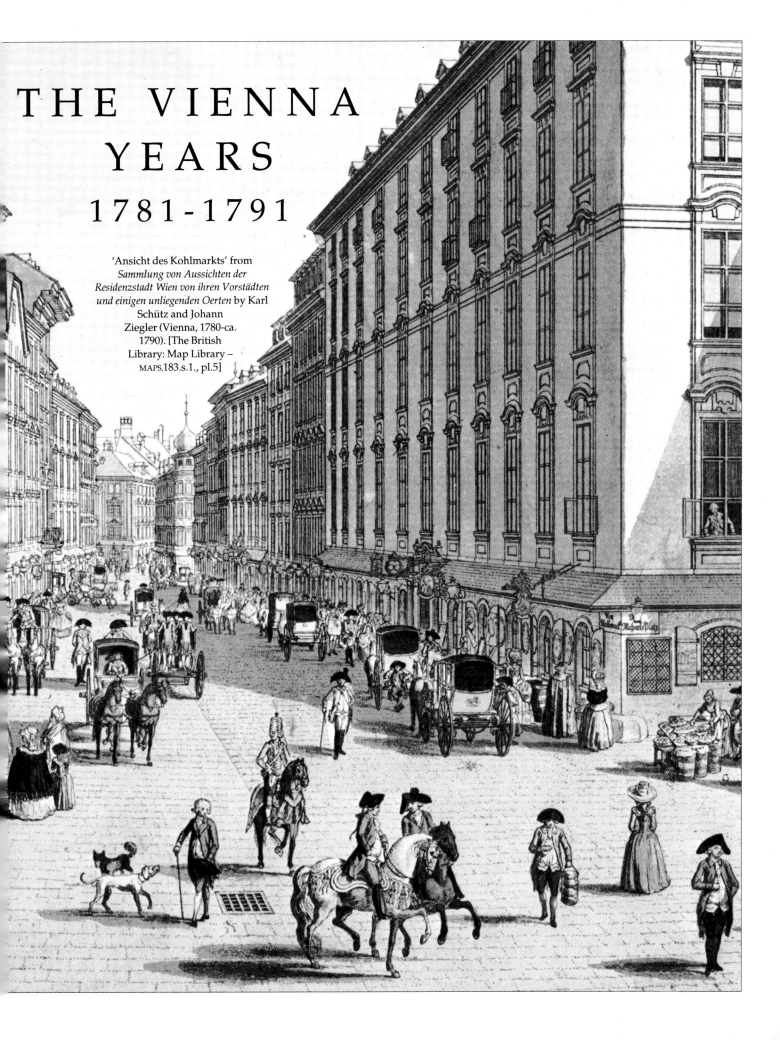

THE VIENNA YEARS

1781-1791

'Ansicht des Kohlmarkts' from *Sammlung von Aussichten der Residenzstadt Wien von ihren Vorstädten und einigen unliegenden Oerten* by Karl Schütz and Johann Ziegler (Vienna, 1780-ca. 1790). [The British Library: Map Library – MAPS.183.s.1., pl.5]

Final split with Colloredo

Mozart arrived in Vienna on 16 March 1781 at 9.00 in the morning. Except for brief trips to Salzburg, Prague, Frankfurt, Berlin, and a few other cities, he would remain in Vienna until his death, in 1791. Colloredo had come to Vienna for the accession, some three months earlier, of Emperor Joseph II. Mozart's arrival was not auspicious. On 17 March, Mozart wrote to his father, who had remained in Salzburg, describing a lunch at the Archbishop's house, where he was staying:

By the way, the two valets sit at the top of the table, but at least I have the honour of being placed above the cooks. Well, I almost believe myself back in Salzburg!

This is Mozart's first letter home after coming to Vienna; it begins 'Mon trés cher amy', a salutation unique in Mozart's correspondence with his father. Unfortunately, not one of Leopold's letters to his son survives from Mozart's Vienna years.

The move to Vienna cannot have been easy for either father or son, and Mozart's letters during his first months there are among the most impassioned and personal that he wrote. Mozart was at once liberated from Colloredo's oppressive restrictions and from Leopold's (understandably) firm paternal hand; his letters, while often contradictory from one sentence to the next, evince a sense of release in his newly found freedom. On 16 May he wrote:

God knows how hard it is for me to leave you; but, even if I had to beg, I could never serve such a master again; for, as long as I live, I shall never forget what has happened. I implore you, I adjure you, by all you hold dear in this world, to strengthen me in this resolution instead of trying to dissuade me from it, for if you do you will only make me unproductive. My desire and my hope is to gain honour, fame, and money, and I have every confidence that I shall be more useful to you in Vienna than if I were to return to Salzburg.

And it is obvious from Mozart's reply three days later that Leopold vehemently disapproved of his son's decision to break with the Archbishop and remain in Vienna. Leopold appealed to Mozart's sense of duty, but his son countered that he was unwilling to compromise his honour:

You say that the only way to save my honour is to abandon my resolve. How can you perpetrate such a contradiction! When you wrote this you surely did not bear in mind that such a recantation would prove me to be the basest fellow in the world. All Vienna knows that I have left the Archbishop, and all Vienna knows the reason! Everyone knows that it was because my honour was insulted — and, what is more, insulted three times. Am I to make myself out to be a cowardly sneak and the Archbishop a worthy prince? No one would like to do the former, and I least of all; and the latter God alone can accomplish, if it be His will to enlighten him . . . To please you, my most beloved father, I would sacrifice my happiness, my health and my life. But my honour — *that* I prize, and you too must prize it, above everything. (19 May 1781)

Mozart turned to composing straightaway. He dated the Rondo for horn and orchestra, K.371, 'Vienne ce 21 mars 1781' (26). This lovely work survives only in Mozart's partially orchestrated draft. Until recently it was thought to be a complete draft, but a few years ago four previously unknown pages of the draft, extending the Rondo by some 60 measures, came to light. Dated just five days after Mozart arrived in Vienna, the Rondo may belong with another fragmentary work, K.370b, presumably the first movement of a horn concerto in E flat. If the two movements do indeed go together, they would form part

26 Mozart's Rondo for horn and orchestra in B flat major, K.371. First page of the partially orchestrated draft, dated 21 March 1781, just five days after Mozart arrived in Vienna. [From The Robert Owen Lehman Collection, on deposit in The Pierpont Morgan Library]

of Mozart's earliest horn concerto, predating the four with which he is generally credited.

In early May, Mozart moved to the home of the Webers *(27)*, whom he had known in Mannheim. Having failed to win the affections of Aloysia Weber (who in the meantime had married the actor Joseph Lange), he now turned his attention to her younger sister Constanze. Mozart dismissed rumours about their relationship as

entirely groundless . . . Because I am living with them [the Webers], therefore I am going to marry the daughter (25 July 1781)

and in early September, at Leopold's urging, he moved again. (Altogether, Mozart lived in eleven residences during his nearly eleven years in Vienna.)

Mozart's six violin sonatas, published in November 1781 as op. II, were his entry into Viennese musical life *(28)*. One of the sonatas, K.296, had been written in Mannheim in 1778; another, K.378/317d, was written either in Salzburg or after his arrival in Vienna in 1781; the other four were composed in Vienna in the summer of that year. What pleases us so deeply in these sonatas (especially the four later ones) is how unerringly Mozart grasps the potential of the medium; how, as later in the 'Haydn' Quartets, he has suddenly moved from the respectable but occasionally commonplace earlier works in the genre to that consummate synthesis of inspiration and expression that characterizes the best works of his maturity. A perceptive review of the sonatas, published in April

27 'Ansicht des Platzes und der Kirche von St Peter', from *Sammlung von Aussichten der Residenzstadt Wien von ihren Vorstädten und einigen unliegenden Oerten* by Karl Schütz and Johann Ziegler (Vienna, 1780-ca.1790). The Webers lived in a house called 'The Eye of God'. [The British Library: Map Library – MAPS.183.s.1., pl.7]

1783 in Cramer's *Magazin der Musik*, begins to take their measure:

These sonatas are unique in their kind. Rich in new ideas and traces of their author's great musical genius. Very brilliant, and suited to the instrument. At the same time the violin accompaniment is so ingeniously combined with the clavier part that both instruments are constantly kept in equal prominence; so that these sonatas call for as skilled a violinist as a clavier player. However, it is impossible to give a full description of this original work. Amateurs and connoisseurs should first play them through for themselves, and they will then perceive that we have in no way exaggerated.[13]

Major operatic success — Die Entführung

During the latter part of 1781 and the early part of 1782 Mozart wrote *Die Entführung aus dem Serail*, to a libretto by Gottlieb Stephanie the younger. The première took place on 16 July 1782 at the Burgtheater which, with the Kärntnerthortheater, was one of the two Imperial theatres (which also served as opera houses) in Vienna. 'Too beautiful for our ears, and far too many notes, my dear Mozart', Joseph II reportedly commented after the first performance; Mozart is said to have replied, 'Exactly as many, Your Majesty, as are needed'. *Die Entführung* was the first great *Singspiel* — German opera with spoken dialogue — and Mozart's first major operatic success; it was performed 34 times in Vienna through 1788, by which time German opera had given way to Italian at the Burgtheater. *Die Entführung* was an epochal work that laid the foundations for many later operas, such as Beethoven's *Fidelio* and Weber's *Freischütz* and *Euryanthe*. When Weber conducted *Die Entführung* in Dresden in 1818, he said that it depicted

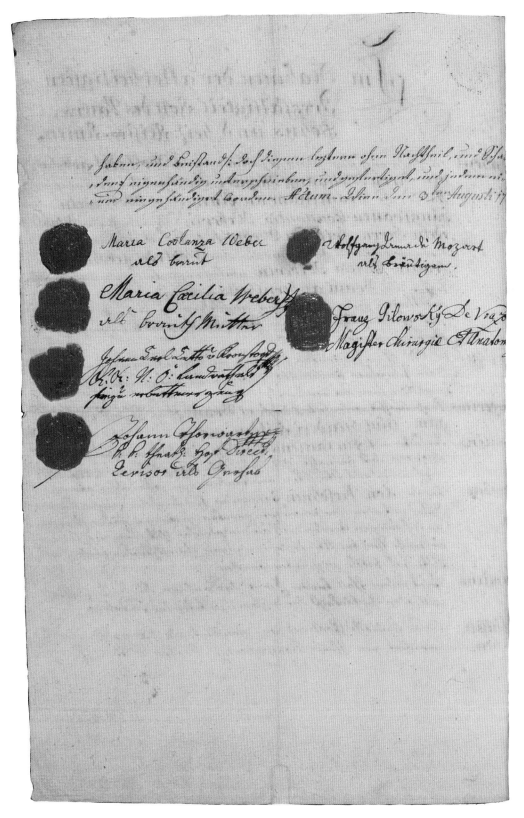

PLATE VI Mozart's marriage contract, dated 3 August 1782, signed by Maria Costanza Weber as the bride, Wolfgang Amadè Mozart as the bridegroom, Maria Cecilia Weber as the bride's mother, two witnesses, and Johann Thorwalt as the bride's guardian. [The British Library: Department of Manuscripts – Zweig 69]

PLATE VII 'Die Metropolitankirche zum Heil: Stephan in Wien', from *Sammlung von Aussichten der Residenzstadt Wien von ihren Vorstädten und einigen unliegenden Oerten* by Karl Schütz and Johann Ziegler (Vienna, 1780-ca.1790). Having signed the contract of marriage on 3 August 1782 Mozart and Constanze were married in St Stephen's Cathedral the following day. [The British Library: Map Library – MAPS.183.s.1., pl.9]

what every man's joyous, youthful years are to him, years the bloom of which he will never recapture . . . I venture to say that in *Die Entführung* Mozart had attained the peak of his artistic experience, to which only experience of the world had to be added later . . . With the best will in the world, he could never have written another *Entführung*.[14]

In December 1781, Mozart had declared his intention to marry Constanze Weber. To his father, he described her as

the martyr of the family and, probably for that very reason, is the kindest-hearted, the cleverest and, in short, the best [of all the daughters] . . . She is not ugly, but at the same time far from beautiful. Her whole beauty consists in two little black eyes and a pretty figure. She has no wit, but she has enough common sense to enable her to fulfil her duties as a wife and mother. It is a downright lie that she is inclined to be extravagant . . . She understands housekeeping and has the kindest heart in the world. I love her and she loves me with all her heart. Tell me whether I could wish myself a better wife? (15 December 1781)

They were married on 4 August 1782 (PLATES VI and VII).

The Rondo for piano and orchestra, K.386, is dated Vienna, 19 October 1782. An autograph of the Rondo, lacking its final leaves, was among the Mozart manuscripts that Constanze sold to the publisher Johann Anton André in 1799. In 1838, Cipriani Potter, the English composer and pianist, published a reduction of the Rondo for piano solo, clearly based on the manuscript, adding an

28 Mozart's Violin Sonata in F major, K.376. First page of the autograph manuscript. One of the six sonatas published in November 1781, the first of Mozart's works published in Vienna after his arrival there. [The Pierpont Morgan Library: Mary Flagler Cary Music Collection.]

29 Mozart's Concert Rondo for piano and orchestra in A major, K.386. Autograph manuscript of part of the long-lost ending of the Rondo. This manuscript had for many years been attributed to Franz Xaver Süssmayr; it was identified as Mozart's autograph only in 1980. [The British Library: Department of Manuscripts – Add. MS 32181]

ending of his own composition to make up for the missing music. The subsequent owner of the manuscript, William Sterndale Bennett, gave away a number of leaves. In 1980, while examining a volume of music manuscripts in the British Library attributed to Franz Xaver Süssmayr, the Austrian composer who completed Mozart's Requiem, Alan Tyson discovered the last three leaves of Mozart's autograph (29). (Some leaves of the manuscript are still missing; what survives is now found in collections from London to Tokyo.) It has been suggested that the Rondo was planned as part of the Piano Concerto in A, K.414/385p, but it seems more likely that Mozart intended it as an independent piece.[15]

In July 1782 Leopold wrote from Salzburg, requesting some music for the ennoblement of Sigmund Haffner, a childhood friend of Mozart's. Mozart replied:

Well, I am up to the eyes in work, for by Sunday week I have to arrange my opera [*Die Entführung*] for wind-instruments. If I don't, someone will anticipate me and secure the profits. And now you ask me to write a new symphony! How on earth can I do so? (20 July 1782)

Mozart sent off the movements of the 'new symphony' piecemeal to Salzburg; the work — minus the opening March, and with flutes and clarinets added — would become the 'Haffner' Symphony (30).[16] (There were no clarinets in the Salzburg orchestra; Mozart's first symphony to include them was K.297, composed in 1778 for the Concert Spirituel, in Paris. The 'Paris' and 'Haffner' Symphonies, both in D major, are scored for the same instruments — pairs of flutes, oboes, clarinets, bassoons, horns, and trumpets, plus timpani and strings — and are his only symphonies written for just those forces.) The four-movement 'Haffner' Symphony was performed at Mozart's first public concert in Vienna, on 23 March 1783, with Joseph II in attendance. Mozart wrote only six symphonies during his 10 years in Vienna: the 'Haffner', the 'Linz', the 'Prague', and those in E flat major, G minor, and C major (the 'Jupiter'); of these, the 'Haffner' was the only one to be published (in 1785) in his lifetime.

Salzburg 1783

Mozart and his wife spent the summer of 1783 in Salzburg, where Leopold and Nannerl met Constanze for the first time. According to anecdote, Michael Haydn (Joseph Haydn's younger brother who, after Mozart broke with Colloredo, assumed Mozart's position as cathedral organist in Salzburg) had been commissioned to compose six duets for violin and viola. Prevented by illness from completing all six, Haydn sought Mozart's assistance; Mozart complied, composing the Duos, K.423-K.424 *(31)*. (Because the Duos are written on Viennese paper, we are not sure whether they were in fact written in Salzburg; perhaps they were composed after Mozart's return to Vienna.) If they are little

30 Mozart's Symphony in D major, K.385. First page of the autograph manuscript of the 'Haffner' Symphony; the flute and clarinet parts, which were added later, can be seen at the top and bottom of the score, written in lighter ink. The symphony was performed on 23 March 1783 at Mozart's first public concert in Vienna. [The Pierpont Morgan Library: Mary Flagler Cary Music Collection]

31 Mozart's Duos for violin and viola, K.423-424. First page of the autograph manuscript. The Duos were composed at the request of Michael Haydn, who had been prevented by illness from completing a commission. [From The Robert Owen Lehman Collection, on deposit in The Pierpont Morgan Library]

performed today it is only because of the unusual combination of instruments; they are mature Mozart in full command of the medium, comparable in invention and freshness to the contemporaneous string quartets.

The Mass in C minor, K.427/417a, was performed in Salzburg on 26 October 1783; Constanze may have sung the soprano solos. Religious music played a very small part in Mozart's life during his Vienna years. The two major liturgical compositions from the period — the Mass, and the Requiem, K.626 — were both left incomplete. For all its occasional beauty, Mozart made few innovations in this music — indeed, it is notable more for its nearly perfect evocation of Baroque style than for any profoundly original musical thought. And while we would be the poorer without the noble torsos (to borrow Alfred Einstein's term) of the Mass and Requiem, some isolated movements from other works, such as the haunting 'Laudate Dominum' from the Solemn Vespers (K.339), and *Ave verum corpus* (K.618), that exquisite gem from his last year, the greatness of Mozart's legacy, unlike Bach's, would be little diminished had he never composed a note for the Church.

Return to Vienna, via Linz

Mozart returned to Vienna by way of Linz (PLATE VIII) where, in early November, he composed the symphony named for that city, K.425, in three days. Near

32 Mozart's Fugue for two pianos in C minor, K.426. First page of the autograph manuscript. [From The Robert Owen Lehman Collection, on deposit in The Pierpont Morgan Library]

the end of December, he wrote the Fugue for two pianos, K.426 *(32)*, one of only two completed works for two pianos (the other being the brilliant Sonata in D major, K.448/375a), and his only keyboard fugue of any distinction, whose contrapuntal intricacies are lost when, as is too often the case, it is played too fast. (On 20 April 1782, Mozart wrote to his sister that 'if a fugue is not played slowly, the ear cannot clearly distinguish the theme when it comes in and consequently the effect is entirely missed'.) If fugal technique came to Mozart with little effort, the inspiration to create memorable music at the same time generally did not. Unlike his models, Bach and Handel, the simultaneous generation of both commanding music and intricate counterpoint seemed to elude him. He mastered the rules, but not always the art, of the fugue. (That he could devise complex polyphony in the service of great music is demonstrated, for example, in the finales of the String Quartet in G, K.387, and of the 'Jupiter' Symphony. But these works were written on his own terms, not on those of his Baroque predecessors.) In 1788, Mozart arranged the Fugue, K.426 *(45)*, for string quartet (or string orchestra), adding an introductory Adagio.

Mozart composed or completed six piano concertos in 1784, four of them (K.449, K.450, K.451, and K.453) between 9 February and 12 April. If such feverish creativity seems remarkable, we should bear in mind that during those nine weeks Mozart wrote the Quintet for piano and winds in E flat, K.452

33 *Verzeichnüss aller meiner Werke*, Mozart's own thematic catalogue of his works written between February 1784 and November 1791. On the left are the dates, the titles of the works, the instruments called for, and, for operas, the singers' names; on the right are the opening bars of the work (in piano reduction where necessary). The five works shown in this opening are the Piano Concerto in E flat, K.482; *Der Schauspieldirektor*, K.486; the Piano Concerto in A, K.488; and a duet (K.489) and aria (K.490) for his opera *Idomeneo*, K.366. [The British Library: Department of Manuscripts – Zweig 63 ff.6ᵛ-7ʳ]

34 Mozart's Piano Concerto in C major, K.467. First page of the autograph manuscript. The first movement is rare in Mozart's autographs in that it lacks a tempo direction, which is found only in the *Verzeichnüss*. [The Pierpont Morgan Library: Dannie and Hettie Heineman Collection]

(which he considered 'the best work I have ever composed'), gave lessons nearly every morning, and, in the evenings, performed in no fewer than 24 concerts. During the year the Mozarts also moved twice. Carl Thomas, their second child (and the first to survive infancy), was born on 21 September 1784. On 11 February 1785, Leopold Mozart came to Vienna, where he stayed until 25 April; it was the last time father and son would be together.

Keeping track of compositions — the Verzeichnüss

On 9 February 1784, Mozart began a thematic catalogue of his works; this *Verzeichnüss aller meiner Werke* is at once an invaluable source for establishing the chronology of his compositions and a precious personal relic (PLATE XI, *33, 48*). The dates in the *Verzeichnüss* must be read with caution; they refer, in most cases, not to the date on which a work was begun or written, but the date on (or near) which it was completed. For example, the very first work entered in the *Verzeichnüss*, the Piano Concerto in E flat, K.449, is dated 9 February 1784, but it was begun in the second half of 1782 — over a year earlier — and only completed in late 1783 or early 1784. The C major Piano Concerto, K.503, dated 4 December 1786 in the *Verzeichnüss*, was apparently begun some two years before. And he seems to have started work on the 'Coronation' Piano Concerto, K.537, dated 24 February 1788, a year or so earlier.

Mozart completed the great Piano Concerto in C, K.467, on 9 March 1785 *(34)*. For richness and diversity of melodic and motivic material, the first movement has few parallels among the concertos. In the outer movements the piano part makes formidable demands on the soloist's technique — C. M. Girdlestone calls one passage in the first movement 'the thickest scrub of arpeggios and broken octaves that Mozart has ever set up before his execu- tants'[17] — but the virtuosity is always at the service of the music and never suggests self-indulgent display. Never, that is, so long as conductor and pianist choose a sensible tempo. The first movement is rare in Mozart's autographs in that it lacks a tempo direction. The first edition, published in 1800, prescribed 'Allegro', as did the *Neue Mozart-Ausgabe*, in 1961 (later corrected in the *Kritische Bericht*). For the true tempo marking we must go to the *Verzeichnüss*, where we find 'Allegro maestoso'. The sustained reverie of the second movement *(35)* is justly famous, and has survived the myriad adaptations and transcriptions — including koto ensemble — to which it has latterly been subjected. It possesses the noble bearing of an aria from the later operas or of a late symphonic slow movement (the Andante cantabile of the 'Jupiter' comes to mind).

Between late March and early June, Mozart composed five songs, including 'Das Veilchen', K.476 *(36)*. In the spring he also wrote some Masonic music, the brooding Fantasy in C minor for piano, K.475, and the cantata *Davidde penitente*, the music for which was largely adapted from the Kyrie and Gloria of the C minor Mass, K.427/417a. Few works are recorded from the summer and autumn. (The Piano Quartet in G minor, K.478, is entered under July in his *Verzeichnüss*, but the autograph is dated 6 October 1785.)

In September 1785, the Vienna firm of Artaria, Mozart's major publisher during his lifetime, issued the six string quartets dedicated to Joseph Haydn (PLATE IX). In the famous dedicatory letter to Haydn, which appears only in the first edition, Mozart refers to the quartets as 'these six children of mine', and expresses the hope that 'they will not seem to you altogether unworthy of your favour . . .'. Haydn had heard the first three quartets performed by Mozart

35 Mozart's Piano Concerto in C major, K.467. First page of the autograph manuscript of the second movement. [The Pierpont Morgan Library: Dannie and Hettie Heineman Collection]

36 'Das Veilchen', K.476. The first page of the autograph manuscript of Mozart's most famous song. The text, by Goethe, tells of a violet that stands in a meadow, expressing the hope that it might be picked by an approaching shepherdess; instead, the maiden steps on the violet, which falls and dies, but nonetheless rejoices: 'Although I die, I do so because of her, because of her, at her feet'. [The British Library: Department of Manuscripts – Zweig 56]

37 Title-page of the first edition of the 'Haydn' quartets (Vienna, 1785). [The British Library: Music Library – R.M.11.g.17.(1.)]

and friends on 15 January 1785 and, four weeks later, the second three. It was after the latter performance, on 12 February, that Haydn made to Leopold Mozart (preserved in a letter Leopold wrote to his daughter) a comment that, two centuries later, resonates with the truth of the moment and the judgment of posterity:

Before God and as an honest man I tell you that your son is the greatest composer known to me either in person or by name. He has taste and, what is more, the most profound knowledge of composition. (16 February 1785)

Mozart had worked on these quartets for about two and a half years, and it is clear from the autographs, and from various rejected sketches and drafts, that they did not come easily. Mozart himself called them 'il frutto di una lunga e laboriosa fatica' (the fruit of long and laborious endeavour), which contradicts the widely held view that he generally wrote quickly and with ease. (He did, of course, do so elsewhere.) Artaria's publication does full justice to the quartets. The elegant engraving of the title page (37), dedicatory letter, and music are altogether worthy of Mozart's creative efforts; both the compositions and their publication bear eloquent testimony to Mozart's deep admiration for Haydn, and stand as moving witness to the relationship between two masters.

38 Mozart's *Der Schauspieldirektor*, K.486. First page of the autograph manuscript of the *Singspiel*. [The Pierpont Morgan Library: Mary Flagler Cary Music Collection]

Commission from Emperor Joseph II— *Der Schauspieldirektor*

On 7 February 1786, Joseph II presented an evening of entertainment at Schönbrunn, his summer residence near Vienna. The occasion was a reception in honour of Duke Albert of Sachsen-Teschen, the governor-general of the Austrian Netherlands, and his wife, the Archduchess Marie Christine, Joseph's sister. The Emperor had commissioned two works to be performed that evening: an *opera buffa* by Antonio Salieri and a *Singspiel* (a play with music) by Mozart. They were given in the Orangery at Schönbrunn, an enormous room nearly 600 feet long and 32 feet wide, with a stage at either end, one for plays, one for operas, filled with rare plants and fruit trees (and the only hall at Schönbrunn which would have been warm enough for such midwinter entertainment). Salieri's contribution to the evening was *Prima la musica e poi le parole* — a work all but forgotten today (although Richard Strauss's last opera, *Capriccio*, is loosely based on the same story).

The libretto for Mozart's *Singspiel*, *Der Schauspieldirektor (38)* was Gottlieb Stephanie, who is remembered mainly as the librettist for *Die Entführung aus dem Serail*. The plot concerns an actor, Puf, and his manager, Frank the impresario, and their attempts to assemble a company of actors for a performance in

Salzburg. Mozart composed the music, comprising an overture, two arias, a trio, and a finale, between 18 January and 3 February — that is, in a little over two weeks. The first critical mention of the work is found in the diary of Count Carl von Zinzendorf, a member and indefatigable chronicler of the court circle in Vienna; he described the splendid Orangery, called *Der Schauspieldirektor* thoroughly mediocre, and failed to mention either Mozart or Salieri by name. The first public performance of the two operas was on 11 February at the Kärntnerthortheater. Mozart's work was well received and was repeated on the 18th and the 25th; these were the only performances during his lifetime.

Collaboration with Lorenzo Da Ponte — Le nozze di Figaro

On 11 November 1785, Leopold Mozart wrote to his daughter:

At last I have received a letter of twelve lines from your brother, dated November 2nd. He begs to be forgiven [for not writing], as he is up to the eyes in work at his opera 'Le Nozze di Figaro' . . . I know the piece; it is a very tiresome play and the translation from the French will certainly have to be altered very freely, if it is to be effective as an opera. God grant that the text may be a success. I have no doubt about the music.

Leopold was perhaps too severe on the play, and, in the event, need not have worried about the libretto: both Beaumarchais's *La folle journée, ou Le mariage de Figaro* and Lorenzo Da Ponte's *Le nozze di Figaro* are counted among the exemplars of their respective genres — as, needless to say, is Mozart's opera. It has been observed that Da Ponte had the rare good fortune to be in the right place at the right time, and we can only guess what direction the history of opera might have taken had he not been in Vienna in 1783. Joseph II, who had long exercised rigid authority over the management of the Burgtheater, was about to revive the Italian opera there and was in need of a dramatist. Da Ponte applied for the post and Joseph accepted him. (At their first meeting, when asked by Joseph II how many plays he had written, Da Ponte replied, 'None, Sire.' 'Good! Good!' Joseph replied with a smile, 'we shall have a virgin muse'.)[18]

Figaro is, among other things, about love and desire in their many guises (and, especially in Act IV, disguises), and it is Cherubino, in 'Non so più cosa son' *(39)* who first uses the word 'amore' — the first of over 50 uses in the libretto of 'amore', 'amare', 'amante', 'amoroso', 'amatore', and 'amabile'. (There are over 60 uses of the French equivalents in Beaumarchais.) In a libretto for a 1788 performance of *Figaro* in Florence, 'Non so più' was replaced by a short aria for Susanna beginning 'Senza speme ognor s'aggira'. And a libretto for a Monza performance in 1787 shows an odder change: the Count enters as usual, just as Susanna has hidden Cherubino behind the chair — and sings 'Voi che sapete', Cherubino's own Act II arietta, with the text altered to reflect the Count's more seasoned ways. It was Beaumarchais, incidentally, in the preface to his play, who insisted that the part be played by 'a young and very pretty woman; we have no very young men in our theatre who are at the same time sufficiently mature to appreciate the fine points of the part'.

Nothing is known about the occasion for which Mozart arranged 'Non so più' for soprano, violin, and piano *(40)*. We may imagine that he found himself with the requisite performers at hand, and quickly produced the *pièce d'occasion*. It is unique among the works of Mozart, being the only complete arrangement of an operatic aria he is known to have made. *Le nozze di Figaro* was first performed on 1 May 1786, and was given nine more times that year.

39 Mozart's draft of the aria 'Non so
più cosa son' from *Le nozze di Figaro,*
K.492. First page of the autograph
manuscript. [The British Library:
Department of Manuscripts – Zweig 57]

In his *Verzeichnüss*, with the date 26 June 1786, Mozart has entered 'Ein Waldhorn Konzert für den Leitgeb'. It seems likely that Mozart's four completed horn concertos (as well as the fragmentary Rondo, K.371, mentioned above) were written for Joseph Leutgeb (*ca.* 1745-1811), an Austrian horn player of exceptional skill. (In 1770, after a concert in Paris, the *Mercure de France* praised his ability to 'sing an adagio as perfectly as the most mellow, interesting, and accurate voice'.)[19] He was, apparently, a musician of more proficiency than culture, and in the manuscripts of the concertos Mozart makes many jokes at his expense. The six surviving leaves of the autograph of K.495 (PLATE X) are written in red, blue, green, and black ink; at the end of the slow movement each letter in the word 'Fine' is written using a different color. But despite all the sarcasm directed at Leutgeb in the manuscripts, Mozart's letters reveal that both Leopold and Mozart had genuine affection for him: Leopold lent him money in 1777 when he opened a cheesemongers shop near Vienna; Mozart twice took him to see *Die Zauberflöte* in 1791; and, in his last surviving letter, Mozart writes that Leutgeb 'is staying to supper with me'. (14 October 1791)

Two Prague visits 1787 — Don Giovanni

In January 1787, Mozart travelled to Prague for the first time; on the 17th he attended, and on the 22nd conducted, a performance of *Figaro*; on the 19th he conducted his Symphony in E flat, K.504 (the 'Prague'). He returned to Vienna in mid-March, and on 4 April wrote his last surviving letter to his father, who died on 28 May. This remarkable document is — his music always excepted — one of the most intensely personal utterances to come from this composer who so often speaks to our most intensely personal selves. Mozart writes:

As death, when we come to consider it closely, is the true goal of our existence, I have formed during the last few years such close relations with this best and truest friend of mankind, that his image is not only no longer terrifying to me, but is indeed very soothing and consoling! And I thank my God for graciously granting me the opportunity (you know what I mean) of learning that death is the *key* which unlocks the door to our true happiness. I never lie down at night without reflecting that — young as I am — I may not live to see another day. (4 April 1787)

Just how uncharacteristic this letter is may be judged by the fact that a recent biographer of Mozart denied that it existed, or at least the possibility that Mozart himself wrote it.

On 1 March 1787, Leopold Mozart wrote a letter to his daughter, Nannerl, in which he mentions 'a little Englishman called Attwood, who was sent to Vienna two years ago for the sole purpose of taking lessons from your brother'. Thomas Attwood (1765-1838), the English composer and organist, lived in Vienna from August 1785 until February 1787. While little is known about the

40 Mozart's arrangement, for voice, violin, and piano, of the aria 'Non so più cosa son' from *Le nozze di Figaro,* K.492. First page of the autograph manuscript. This is the only complete arrangement of an operatic aria Mozart is known to have made. [The Pierpont Morgan Library: Dannie and Hettie Heineman Collection]

instruction Mozart gave his other pupils, Attwood was surely the most gifted of them; he received the most extensive tutelage, and so far as we know he was the only pupil to be instructed in both music theory and free composition. Fortunately, the priceless record of Mozart's instruction survives in the so-called 'Attwood Manuscript' *(41)*, a volume of nearly 300 pages, with music and text on 267 pages: twelve are in Mozart's hand, 140 in Attwood's, and 115 have the handwriting of both. Mozart liked and admired Attwood; in his *Reminiscences*, published in 1826, Michael Kelly (who sang the parts of Bartolo and Basilio in the première of *Figaro*, in 1786) recalled Mozart's impression of his pupil: 'Attwood is a young man for whom I have a sincere affection and esteem; he conducts himself with great propriety, and I feel much pleasure in telling you, that he partakes more of my style than any scholar I ever had; and I predict, that he will prove a sound musician.'[20]

On 1 October 1787, Mozart left for his second trip to Prague where, on the 29th, he conducted the première of *Don Giovanni*. It is not *opera seria* — the music (that is, the drama) moves much too fast: no *opera seria* opens with the headlong

dramatic (that is, musical) urgency of the opera's first ten minutes. Nor is it *opera buffa*, in which a murder at the beginning and the protagonist's descent in Hell at the end would have no conceivable place. Mozart, in his *Verzeichnüss*, called it an *opera buffa*; Da Ponte, using Carlo Goldoni's term, called it a *dramma giocoso*, literally 'jocular drama' but a term that defies easy translation; 'a frolic with serious elements', Daniel Heartz's paraphrase, conveys the genre's unique interplay of the comedic and the serious. Writing in 1754, Goldoni described the genesis of the genre: 'If the drama is a little on the serious side, it is condemned for want of levity; if it is too ridiculous, it is damned for want of nobility. I wished to find the way to content everyone, but finding no models anywhere, I have been forced for the past six years to create them.'[21]

Leporello is defined as a *buffo* character from the first notes that he sings; her vengeance arias mark Donna Anna unmistakably as a *seria* part; Donna Elvira falls between the two (Goldoni's 'parte di mezzo carattere'). Don Ottavio is something of an anomaly, neither *seria* nor *buffo*, a largely ineffectual party to the drama, the mirror image of *Don Giovanni*: Ottavio is faithful, indecisive, and

honourable, Don Giovanni profligate, decisive, and reprobate.[22] Mozart's and Da Ponte's mixture of *seria* and *buffo* is evident throughout the score: the tumultuous opening scenes mentioned above; Leporello's mocking 'Catalogue Aria' which immediately follows Elvira's distress at again encountering Giovanni; Giovanni and Zerlina's flirtatious duet followed by Elvira's angrily declamatory 'Ah fuggi il traditor'; Anna's vendetta aria 'Or sai chi l'onore' followed by the Don's lusty 'Fin ch'an dal vino'; the sudden changes from the courtly Minuet to the ravishing Trio to the festive polymetric preparations for the ball. (The great Sextet in Act II also bears memorable witness to Mozart's musico-dramatic genius.) But it is not simply the intermingling of serio-comic ingredients that gives *Don Giovanni* its extraordinary momentum; Mozart has eliminated anything that might impede the narrative progress, 'and has welded individual scenes and episodes of the story into the broader sweep of the opera. Instead of a genial sequence of memorable but distinct musical experiences [as in *Figaro*], the work is characterized by a powerful unity of purpose.'[23]

Like the other late operas, *Don Giovanni* was the object of intense and often contemptuous criticism, both in its own day and, especially, in the nineteenth century. Two examples will suffice. In 1791 a Berlin reviewer wrote, 'Full of the highest anticipations I went to see and hear a musical drama in which, to my mind, *the eye was feasted, the ear enchanted, reason offended, modesty outraged, and virtue and sensibility trampled upon by vice.*'[24] But the reviewer goes on to praise the music: 'Never has the art of music reached to a higher degree! Melodies which seem to have been invented by an angel are here accompanied by celestial harmonies . . .'[25] And a later writer considered the work 'the foolishest and most monstrous of conceivable human works and subjects of thought. No such spectacle of unconscious . . . moral degradation of the highest faculty to the lowest purpose can be found in history.' While this sounds very much like a fulmination against, say, Strauss's *Salome*, it is, in fact, John Ruskin on *Don Giovanni*.[26]

Vienna, and a position at court

Mozart returned to Vienna in mid-November 1787. In December, Joseph II offered him the position of court *Kammermusicus*, or Court Composer *(42)*. The post required little more than writing dance music for court balls, but did provide him with a salary of 800 gulden, about £8,500 ($16,000) at 1990 rates.[27] Mozart's documented income and expenses have been widely studied. If we add to his recorded earnings the estimated amounts he was paid for his own concerts, subscription concerts, in royalties, and other, miscellaneous, income, it appears that between 1782 and 1791 his average annual income was 3,500 gulden, or £37,000 (about $70,000) in 1990. His annual expenses for those years have been estimated at 2,000 gulden (£21,000, or $40,000). He should, then, have had a net income of about £15,000 ($28,000); but a combination of an extravagant lifestyle and, possibly, substantial gambling debts (the latter are largely undocumented) resulted in frequent and heavy indebtedness. By all accounts, Mozart was certainly not frugal: although his income far exceeded his expenses, he seems never to have saved any money at all. But he was extremely well paid, and if on occasion he found himself in straitened circumstances, they resulted from financial imprudence, not low income. In short, he was neither poor nor poorly paid, just irresponsible.

PLATE VIII 'Ansicht der Stadt Linz' by Joseph & Peter Schaffer, from *Sammlung von Aussichten der Residenzstadt Wien von ihren Vorstädten und einigen unliegenden Oerten* by Karl Schütz and Johann Ziegler (Vienna, 1780-ca.1790). [The British Library: Map Library – MAPS.183.s.1., second supplement, pl.4]

PLATE IX Mozart's String Quartet in C major, K.465. The first page of the autograph manuscript of the 'Dissonance' Quartet, one of the six quartets dedicated to Joseph Haydn. [The British Library: Department of Manuscripts – Add. MS 37763, f.57ʳ]

PLATE X Mozart's Horn Concerto in E flat major, K.495. A page from the only surviving leaves of the autograph manuscript. [The Pierpont Morgan Library: Mary Flagler Cary Music Collection]

PLATE XI 'Verzeichnüss aller meiner Werke'. The five works shown in this opening are the Piano Concerto in D major, K.537 (the 'Coronation'); the soprano aria 'A se in ciel, benigne stelle', K.538; 'Ich möchte wohl der Kaiser sein', K.539, which Mozart calls a 'German war song'; the Adagio for piano in B minor, K.540; and the tenor aria 'Dalla sua pace', K.540a, composed for the first Vienna performance of *Don Giovanni*. [The British Library: Department of Manuscripts – Zweig 63, ff.15ᵛ-16ʳ]

42 Mozart's letter to his sister, Nannerl, dated 19 December 1787. In the letter, he announces that Joseph II has appointed him Court Composer. [The British Library: Department of Manuscripts – Add. MS 41628, f.204]

43   Mozart's Piano Concerto in D major, K.537. First page of the autograph manuscript of the 'Coronation' Concerto. Mozart played the concerto in Dresden in April 1789 and, on 15 October 1790, at celebrations in Frankfurt surrounding the coronation of Leopold II as Holy Roman emperor. [The Pierpont Morgan Library: Dannie and Hettie Heineman Collection]

Mozart's Piano Concerto in D major, K.537, was completed in late February 1788 ((43) and PLATE XI). But a study of the paper-types found in the manuscript shows that it was begun almost a year earlier and that he returned to it only in late 1787 or early 1788. The most notable feature of the manuscript is that the piano part is largely incomplete: there is not a single note written for the left hand in the slow movement (44), and the left-hand piano part is missing in long passages in the first and third movements as well. Mozart played the concerto in Dresden in April 1789 and, on 15 October 1790, at celebrations in Frankfurt surrounding the coronation of Leopold II as Holy Roman emperor. Mozart also performed his Piano Concerto in F, K.459; both concertos have been given the nickname 'Coronation', which is today usually applied only to K.537. (Johann André published both concertos in 1794, with the left-hand piano part of K.537 fully written out. Since there is no evidence that Mozart ever completed the piano part, it is likely that it was reconstructed by André himself, or with the help of a colleague.) The Frankfurt programme lists other works by Mozart, including 'Eine neue grose Symphonie'. It has been claimed that Mozart never heard performances of his last three symphonies, composed in 1788. We do not know which 'new symphony' was played in Frankfurt, but it has been observed that the presumed wind complement of the orchestra there was exactly that of the 'Coronation' Concerto — and, alone among all of Mozart's symphonies,

44 Mozart's Piano Concerto in D major, K.537. First page of the autograph manuscript of the second movement of the 'Coronation' Concerto. Note that only the right hand of the piano part is present; the left-hand part is lacking throughout the movement, and has not been written out in much of the first and third movements as well. [The Pierpont Morgan Library: Dannie and Hettie Heineman Collection]

that of the 'Jupiter' Symphony.[28] The concert was well received but poorly attended, and Mozart earned little money from it.

The first performance of *Don Giovanni* in Vienna was on 7 May 1788, for which Mozart composed Don Ottavio's 'Dalla sua pace' and Donna Elvira's 'In quali eccessi . . . Mi tradì'. In June, July, and August he wrote his last three symphonies, those in E flat major, K.543, G minor, K.550, and C major, K.551 (the 'Jupiter').

Berlin 1789

On 8 April 1789, Mozart left for Berlin with Prince Karl Lichnowsky (to whom Beethoven would later dedicate, among other works, his *Pathétique* Sonata and Second Symphony). Travelling by way of Prague, Dresden, Leipzig, and Potsdam, they arrived in the Prussian capital on 19 May. The reason for this trip is unknown. The Court may have invited Mozart to compose six string quartets (presumably for King Frederick Wilhelm II, a keen cellist — Haydn's op.50 quartets are dedicated to him) and six piano sonatas (perhaps for Princess Friederike, the king's eldest daughter).

Mozart composed three of the quartets — K.575, K.589, and K.590 — which are known today as the 'Prussian' Quartets *(46)*. The paper used in the first two, apparently purchased in Dresden or Prague — that is, during the trip itself —

45 Mozart's Fugue for string quartet (or string orchestra?), K.546, an arrangement of his Fugue for two pianos, K.426 (see fig.32). The upper four staves, in a copyist's hand, contain the original two-piano version; the lower four staves, in Mozart's hand, show his version for strings. The Adagio that Mozart wrote to precede the Fugue is not present in this manuscript. [The British Library: Department of Manuscripts - Add. MS 28966, ff.3ᵛ-4ʳ]

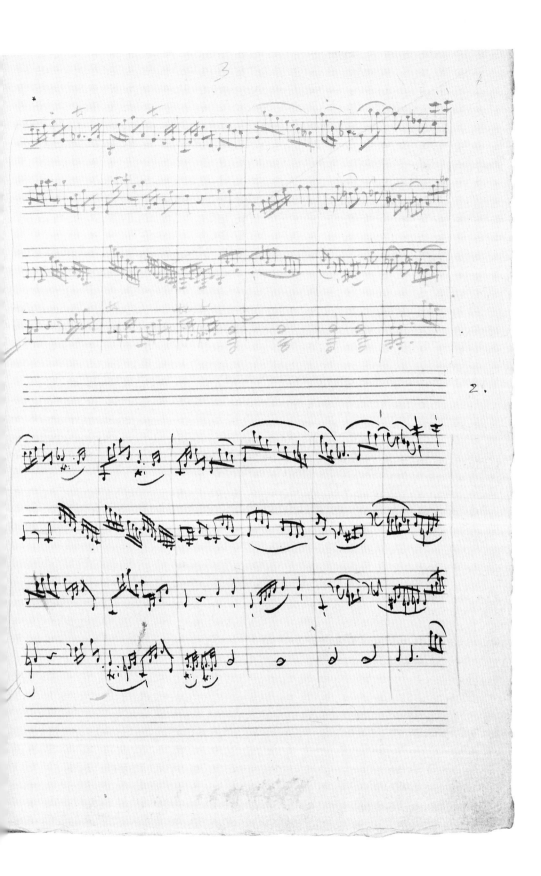

46   Mozart's String Quartet in B flat major, K.589. Opening of the autograph manuscript of the second 'Prussian' Quartet. [The British Library: Department of Mansucripts – Add. MS 37765, f.29ᵀ]

strongly suggests that he was eager to start work on them: all of K.575 and part of K.589 were apparently completed before he returned to Vienna on 4 June, or shortly thereafter. As we have already seen, received opinion has long held that Mozart composed rapidly, with little revision and few second thoughts. But a study of the manuscripts of these three works points to a quite different conclusion: the 'Prussian' Quartets, like the 'Haydn' Quartets of 1783-85, were also clearly 'the fruit of long and laborious endeavour'. Mozart himself, in a letter to his friend and fellow Mason Michael Puchberg, referred to these, his last quartets, as 'diese mühsame Arbeit' ('that exhausting labour'). Several of the movements begin with false starts; and the variety of paper-types and handwriting found in the quartets do not reveal a composer putting on paper music fully formed in his head, but one struggling with the materials of his art.

Mozart never wrote the remaining three quartets for the King; of the six 'leichte Klaviersonate' for the princess he wrote only one, that in D major, K.576. This, the last of Mozart's 19 piano sonatas, is not exactly easy, either in conception or execution, and is musically one of the most satisfying of all his solo piano works. There is some imitative writing in the first movement (quite rare in Mozart's solo keyboard works), an Adagio with the expansive lyricism and dark harmonic contrasts of the piano concerto slow movements, and a concluding rondo of winning grace and *élan*. There are those who, forced to choose their desert-island keyboard sonatas, would with little hesitation take Haydn's before Mozart's (and they might take Haydn's symphonies before Mozart's as well). Their reasons would have little to do with simple numbers (Haydn wrote twice as many sonatas and over 40 more symphonies) but with quality and diversity. There is no lack of invention and pianistic elegance in Mozart's sonatas; what we often miss is the element of surprise, a sense of eager anticipation of what might be next. Mozart often comfortably fulfils our expectations; in Haydn, surprise is always imminent. Haydn's symphonies, taken as a whole, are more interesting than Mozart's, especially those from his Salzburg years: they are by turns stately and impertinent, sophisticated and plainspoken, stirring and irreverent, witty (but never frivolous) and sad (but never solemn). His sonatas contain more variety and are frequently more gratifying to the performer than Mozart's. Our desert-island Crusoe would be denied many wonderful works: Haydn wrote no G minor or 'Jupiter' Symphony, no A minor or B flat (K.333) Piano Sonata; but Mozart never quite equalled Haydn's two E flat sonatas (nos. 49 and 52) or the sheer exuberance of the London Symphonies.

On 29 December 1789, Mozart wrote to Michael Puchberg:

> . . .I invite you, you alone, to come along on Thursday at 10 o'clock in the morning to hear a short rehearsal of my opera. I am only inviting Haydn and yourself.

The opera was *Così fan tutte*. Three weeks later, Mozart invited Haydn to the first instrumental rehearsal at the theatre. (Between rehearsals, on 8 January, Haydn probably heard *Le nozze di Figaro* for the first time.)[29] Unfortunately, although Haydn very likely attended a performance of *Così*, his opinion of it is not recorded.

The première of *Così* was on 26 January 1790 at the Burgtheater. On 5 January the following year, he completed his last piano concerto, that in B flat, K.595. In June he wrote *Ave verum corpus*, K.618, the only religious work he completed during his Vienna years (although many movements from the incomplete liturgical compositions are, of course, longer than K.618), and in July began work on *Die Zauberflöte*. His second surviving son, Franz Xaver Wolfgang, was born on 26 July.

Prague 1791 — a coronation commission

In mid-July 1791, Mozart was commissioned to write an opera for the celebrations surrounding the coronation, in September, of Leopold II as King of Bohemia. Questions remain about when Mozart began composing *La clemenza di Tito (47)*, and how long it took him, but we now know that the often-repeated claim that he finished it in 18 days is wrong. (Mozart did not write the recitatives, which form by far the major part of the text; these have been attributed to Süssmayr.) The libretto, based on Metastasio, was adapted by Caterino Mazzolà; aside from Emanuel Schickaneder (for *Die Zauberflöte*), Mazzolà is the only librettist mentioned by Mozart in his *Verzeichnüss*.

Mozart arrived in Prague, with most of the opera completed, on 28 August. Between then and 6 September he wrote (or possibly rewrote) the Overture and a few other numbers. An examination of the paper-types on which *Tito* is written suggests a familiar pattern: Mozart wrote the ensembles (duets, trios, quintets, etc.) before the arias. The reason for this is simple: as a rule, Mozart did not write the solo numbers of an opera until he had heard the singers who would actually be performing them. There would, for example, be no point in

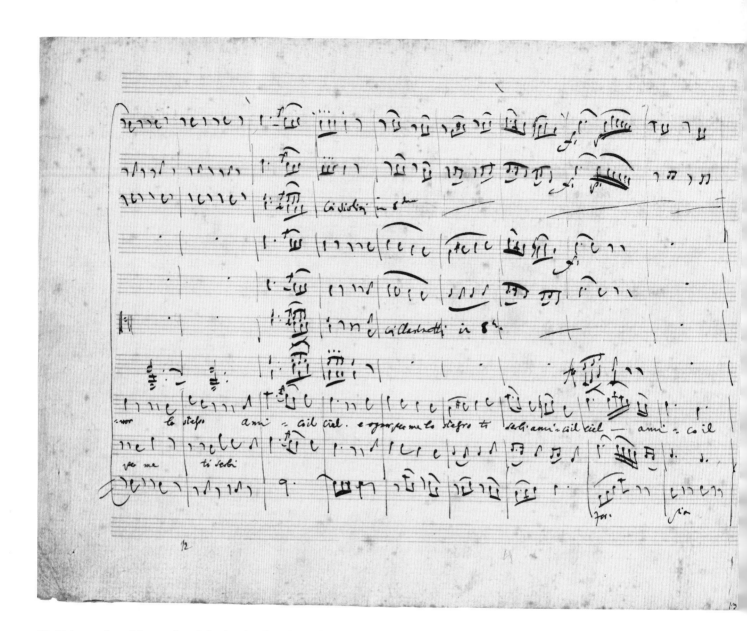

47 'Deh prendi un dolce amplesso', the duettino from Act I of Mozart's *La clemenza di Tito*, K.621. Second and third pages of the autograph manuscript. [The British Library: Department of Manuscripts – Zweig 62]

ciel. — am = ciel ciel.

24
...eggi subito la marcia d...

writing the Queen of Night's arias in *Die Zauberflöte* for a singer who could not negotiate their formidable difficulties; nor would Mozart have written Fiordiligi's 'Come scoglio' in *Così fan tutte* for a soprano who found the sudden changes of register unmanageable. Mozart did, however, write two of Tito's arias while he was at work on the ensembles, but in this case he already knew the singer he was writing for: Antonio Baglioni, the tenor who sang Don Ottavio in the original *Don Giovanni*.

The first performance of *La clemenza di Tito* took place on 6 September at the National Theatre in Prague. Initially, the opera was not well received — the Empress has won a secure if notorious place in the lexicon of musical invective by reportedly calling it 'una porcheria tedesca' (German rubbish) — but at its final performance, on 30 September, it was given 'with tremendous applause'. (7–8 October 1791). Two of the arias — Sesto's 'Parto, ma tu ben mio' and Vitella's celebrated 'Non più di fiori' (the latter probably composed well before the rest of the opera) — have prominent obbligatos for clarinet and basset-horn. They were written for the famous virtuoso Anton Stadler, for whom the Clarinet Quintet, K.581, and Concerto, K.622, were also composed. At the last performance of *Tito* in Prague, cries of 'Bravo!' were shouted at Stadler from the parterre and even from the orchestra. *Tito* was given throughout Europe during the next two decades — it was, with *Die Zauberflöte*, his most popular opera — and, in 1806, was the first of Mozart's operas to be performed in London.

Vienna and Die Zauberflöte

Mozart returned to Vienna in the middle of September. He wrote the Priests' March and Overture for *Die Zauberflöte*, and conducted the première on 30 September at Schickaneder's Theater auf der Wieden. Around the 8th or 9th of October, Mozart wrote to his wife, telling her of a joke he played on Schickaneder, who was performing Papageno:

During Papageno's aria with the glockenspiel ['Ein Mädchen oder Weibchen'] I went behind the scenes, as I felt a sort of impulse today to play it myself. Well, just for fun, at the point where Schickaneder had a pause, I played an arpeggio. He was startled, looked behind the wings and saw me. When he had his next pause, I played no arpeggio. This time he stopped and refused to go on. I guessed what he was thinking and again played a chord. He then struck the glockenspiel and said 'Shut up'. Whereupon everyone laughed. I am inclined to think that this joke taught many of the audience for the first time that Papageno does not play the instrument himself. (8–9 October 1791)

On 14 October, in his last surviving letter, Mozart wrote to Constanze, who was taking the cure at Baden:

At six o'clock [the previous evening] I called in the carriage for Salieri and Madame Cavalieri [Salieri's mistress, and the first Constanze in *Die Entführung*] — and drove them to my box. Then I drove back quickly to fetch Mamma [Mozart's mother-in-law] and Carl Thomas [his elder son], whom I had left at Hofer's. You can hardly imagine how charming they were and how much they liked not only my music, but the libretto and everything. They both said it was an *operone* [a 'grand opera'], worthy to be performed for the grandest festival and before the greatest monarch, and that they would often go to see it, as they had never seen a more beautiful or delightful show. Salieri listened and watched most attentively and from the overture to the last chorus there was not a single number that did not call forth from him a bravo! or bello! It seemed as if they could not thank me enough for my kindness.

The literature on *Die Zauberflöte* is vast, and much of it is concerned with the opera's depiction of Masonic symbolism and beliefs. As early as 1794 it was also seen as an allegory on the French Revolution: 'The basic idea of the opera is: the liberation of the French people from the hands of the old despotism through the wisdom of better legislation'.[30] The Queen of Night was seen as representing the *ancien régime*, Pamina as symbolizing Freedom, Tamino the people, Sarastro the wisdom of better legislation, Papageno the wealthy, the Three Slaves servants and mercenaries of Monostatos, the Three Boys intelligence, justice, and patriotism, and so on. (It might be noted in passing that the playbill for the first performance of the opera individually lists the Three Slaves, speaking parts that are often omitted, but altogether omits the Three Boys, who have prominent singing roles, and some enchanting music, in three numbers, including the two Finales.)

In October, Mozart finished the Clarinet Concerto, K.622; over half of the first movement survives in the draft of an uncompleted basset-horn concerto, written down a year or two before, possibly as early as 1787.[31] In October he also began the Requiem, which had been commissioned in mid-July by Count Walsegg-Stuppach for his wife, who had died in February. He worked on this, his last composition, until 20 November, when, extremely ill, he took to his bed. The Requiem was completed, mostly by Süssmayr, partly by Joseph Eybler, after Mozart's death. It was first performed, in Vienna, on 2 January 1793, in Jahn's hall in the Himmelpfortgasse; probably soon thereafter, Count Walsegg-Stuppach finally received the score of the work he had commissioned 18 months before and, passing it off as his own composition, conducted it on 14 December 1793 in the Neuklosterkirche, Wiener-Neustadt.[32]

Mozart died of chronic renal failure on 5 December 1791, just before 1.00 in the morning; he was 35 years old. Two centuries after the fact, a precise diagnosis of the cause (or causes) of Mozart's death will no doubt always elude us, and each new reading of the symptoms is sure to be challenged as soon as it appears. Recent studies by Peter J. Davies have led him to the hypothesis, based on extensive research and supported by cogent argument, 'that following recurrent streptococcal infections, Mozart developed in turn erythema nodosum, rheumatic fever, and Schönlein-Henoch Syndrome'.[33] He was buried, probably on 6 December, in a common grave at St Marx churchyard, outside Vienna. Mozart's sister, Nannerl, died in Salzburg in 1829 at the age of 78. Of the Mozarts' six children only two survived infancy: Carl Thomas, the second, was born in 1784 and died in 1858 — 67 years after his father; their sixth child, Franz Xaver Wolfgang, was born in 1791, four and a half months before Mozart's death, and died in 1844. Neither son married. Constanze died in 1842, at the age of 80, having survived her first husband by over 50 years and her second, Georg Nikolaus Nissen, by fourteen, one of the first in an illustrious line of composers' widows who long outlived their husbands: Clara Schumann died nearly 40 years after Robert, Cosima Wagner 47 after Richard, Geneviève Bizet 51 after Georges, and Alma Mahler 53 after Gustav. And Camille Saint-Saëns — he was born in 1835, and died in 1921 at the age of 86 — was survived by his wife, who lived until 1950 (he had not seen her since 1881).

Music is anything but a universal language. But Mozart's genius, like Bach's, was to make universal the languages that he knew, which, for Mozart, meant those of the Italian symphony and *opera buffa*, the German *Singspiel*, the string quartets of Haydn, the symphonies and solo concertos of J. C. Bach. He transcended them all: *Le nozze di Figaro* and *Don Giovanni* were unprecedented and had few worthy descendants, and the chamber music and piano concertos from his Vienna years would not be equalled in originality and dramatic force until Beethoven — and some not even then. There are those who would argue — and they would have legions on their side — that there exists no more nearly perfect example of the symphonist's art than the 'Jupiter' Symphony, the last movement of which has without exaggeration been called one of the miracles of Western music.[34] In Mozart's day, the breathtaking polyphony of this movement was not to everyone's taste; in 1798, Carl Friedrich Zelter alleged that in the fugal Finale, 'as we all know, [Mozart] pushed things a little too far'. But then Mozart pushed many things further than his contemporaries. He had an intuitive comprehension of how to design large-scale harmonic structures, and understood the emotional drama that they could generate in the receptive mind. Is there a great composer who did not transcend the formal and expressive boundaries of his day? Monteverdi, Gluck, Beethoven, Schubert, Schumann, Wagner, Mahler, Stravinsky — the list is expandable, but not infinitely so. And few will deny that Mozart, 'that miracle that God let be born in Salzburg', was, among all his contemporaries, the sovereign master of the Viennese classical style and that he brought it to its most glorious fruition.

48 'Verzeichnüss aller meiner Werke' showing the final page of entries that Mozart made. *La Clemenza di Tito* appears between two entries for *Die Zauberflöte,* followed by the Clarinet Concerto and Mozart's last completed work, the Masonic Cantata, K.623. [The British Library: Department of Manuscripts – Zweig MS 63 ff.28ᵛ-29ʳ]

NOTES

1 From Friedrich Wilhelm Marpurg, *Historische-Kritische Beyträge zur Aufnahme der Musik* (Berlin, 1757). English translation from O. E Deutsch, *Mozart: a documentary biography*, translated by E. Blom, P. Branscombe and J. Noble (Stanford and London, 1965 and 1966) p.10.

2 He was baptised Joannes Chrysost[omus] Wolfgangus Theophilus. 27 January was the feast day of St John Chrysostom. The German form of Theophilus is Gottlieb, and the Latin is Amadeus. Mozart was referred to as 'Wolfgang', with various diminutive versions by his parents, and signed himself most often as 'Wolfgango Amadeo' and 'Wolfgang Amadè'.

3 Mozart's works were assigned numbers in Ludwig Ritter von Köchel's *Chronologisch-thematisches Verzeichnis sämtlicher Tonwerke Wolfgang Amadé Mozart* (Leipzig, 1862) [Chronological-Thematic Catalogue of the complete works of Wolfgang Amadé Mozart] and these numbers will be used for each of Mozart's works referred to. Where two numbers are given in the text, the second refers to the number assigned in the 6th edition, edited by F. Giegling, A. Weinmann and G. Sievers (Wiesbaden, 1964), in which the chronology was substantially revised.

4 *Correspondance littéraire, philosophique et critique addressée à un souverain de l'Allemagne* 1 December 1763. The Correspondance was circulated in manuscript by Grimm. English translation from Deutsch, op.cit.

5 A. H. King, *A Mozart legacy: aspects of the British Library collections* (London, 1984) p.20.

6 *Aristide ou le citoyen, Lausanne*, 11 October 1766. Translation from Deutsch, op. cit. p.61.

7 Deutsch, op.cit. p.80.

8 For a detailed discussion of Leopold's list see Neal Zaslaw, 'Leopold Mozart's list of his son's works' in Allan W. Atlas (ed.), *Music in the Classic Period: Essays in Honour of Barry S. Brook* (New York, 1985).

9 Giovanni Battista Martini (1706-84) was an extraordinarily influential Italian writer, teacher and composer to whom many composers turned for tuition and advice, including J. C. Bach and Nicolò Jommelli.

10 Mozart was to make a similar suggestion whilst in Munich in 1780. This is not unlike the scheme which was later to enable Beethoven to remain in Vienna when, after an offer of the post of Kapellmeister to Jerome Bonaparte in Cassel, some of his admirers got together to provide an annual sum to enable him to stay in the city.

11 Founded in 1725 initially for the production of sacred vocal works, though soon being enlarged to include instrumental works.

12 W. A. Mozart, *Sonatas for pianoforte - Sonata in A minor, K.310* ed. Stanley Sadie. Fingering and notes on performance by Denis Matthews (London, 1981).

13 Deutsch, op.cit., p.214.

14 Quoted in Andrew Porter, *Music of Three More Seasons, 1977-1980* (New York, 1981), p.448.

15 This extremely abbreviated account of K.386 is based on Alan Tyson, 'The Rondo for Piano and Orchestra, K.386' in *Mozart: Studies of the Autograph Scores* (Cambridge, Mass., and London, 1987), pp.262- 89.

16 It has long been held that the original Haffner music had two minuets and that Mozart discarded one of them when he turned the work into a symphony. But Neal Zaslaw argues that there was only one minuet to begin with, and that the only movement Mozart dropped was the March. See Neal Zaslaw, *Mozart's Symphonies: Context, Performance Practice, Reception* (Oxford, 1989), p.381.

17 C. M. Girdlestone, *Mozart's Piano Concertos* (London, 1978), p.336.

18 From Da Ponte's *Memoirs*, quoted in Sheila Hodges, *Lorenzo Da Ponte: The Life and Times of Mozart's Librettist* (London, 1985), p.47.

19 Reginald Morley-Pegge, 'Leutgeb [Leitgeb], Joseph,' in S. Sadie (ed.). *The New Grove Dictionary of Music and Musicians* (London, 1980), v.10, p.699.

20 Deutsch, op.cit., p.531.

21 Daniel Heartz, 'Goldoni, Don Giovanni and the dramma giocoso', *The Musical Times*, 120 (1979), p.993.

22 Andrew Steptoe, *The Mozart-Da Ponte Operas: The Cultural and Musical Background to Le nozze di Figaro, Don Giovanni, and Così fan tutte* (Oxford, 1990), p.210.

23 Ibid., p.185.

24 Deutsch, op.cit., p.391.

25 Ibid., p.392.

26 Quoted in Steptoe, op.cit., p.6.

27 It has been estimated that during the Josephine decade (1780-1790), the gulden was equivalent to $20 (about £10.50) in 1990. Volkmar Braunbehrens, *Mozart in Vienna: 1781-1791*, trans. Timothy Bell (New York and London, 1990), pp.132-33.

28 Zaslaw, *Mozart's Symphonies*, p.429.

29 H. C. Robbins Landon, *Haydn: Chronicle and Works. Vol. 2: Haydn at Eszterháza, 1766-1790* (Bloomington and London, 1978), pp.734-35.

30 Quoted in Braunbehrens, op.cit., p.396.

31 Tyson, op.cit., p.35.

32 Paul Moseley, 'Mozart's Requiem: A Revaluation of the Evidence', *Journal of the Royal Musical Association*, 114 (1989), p.216.

33 Peter J. Davies, *Mozart in Person: His Character and Health* (New York, 1989), p.205.

34 Zaslaw, *Mozart's Symphonies*, p.442.

MOZART AUTOGRAPHS
IN THE BRITISH LIBRARY, LONDON AND
THE PIERPONT MORGAN LIBRARY, NEW YORK.

LIST OF COLLECTION NAMES

Cary Mary Flagler Cary Music Collection in The Pierpont Morgan Library

Heineman Dannie and Hettie Heineman Collection in The Pierpont Morgan Library

Lehman Deposit Robert Owen Lehman Collection, on deposit in The Pierpont Morgan Library

Koch The Frederick R. Koch Foundation Collection, on deposit in The Pierpont Morgan Library

MFC Mary Flagler Cary Music Collection in The Pierpont Morgan Library

Morgan The Pierpont Morgan Library

Add. MS The British Library, Department of Manuscripts, Additional Manuscript

Zweig Stephan Zweig collection in The British Library, Department of Manuscripts

K.... The British Library, Music Library

THE AUTOGRAPHS

Arranged by K^6 numbers

K.1a-d   Earliest compositions, in the hand of Leopold Mozart
Cary 201

K.20   Four-part chorus, 'God is our Refuge'. Partly in Leopold Mozart's hand.
K.10 a 17.(3.)

K.40   Cadenza for a concerto movement for piano and orchestra, adapted from a sonata by Leontzi Honauer.
Add. MS 47861A, f.10^r

K.112   Symphony in F major. Full score; the Menuet (but not the Trio) is in Leopold Mozart's hand.
Heineman MS 153

K.381/123a   Sonata for piano duet in D major. Pages 11 and 12 of 13 pages.
Cary 336

K.184/161a   Symphony in E-flat major.

Full score. The first two pages of the first movement are in the hand of Leopold Mozart, and the reaminder of the movement is in the hand of a copyist; the second and third movements are in the hand of Wolfgang Amadeus.
Lehman Deposit

K.199/161b   Symphony in G major. Full score.
Lehman Deposit

K.162   Symphony in C major. Full score.
Lehman Deposit

K.181/162b   Symphony in D major. Full score.
Lehman Deposit

K.168   String Quartet in F major. Fragment of a possibly earlier version of the minuet, K.168a
Add. MS 47861A, f.10^v

K.172   String Quartet in B flat major.
Add. MS 31749.

K.173   String Quartet in D minor. Draft of part of the last movement.
Zweig MS 52

K.182/173dA   Symphony in B flat major. Full score.
Lehman Deposit

K.183/173dB   Symphony in G minor. [In the hand of Leopold Mozart:] Full score.
Lehman Deposit

K.176   Minuet no.3, and trio, no.6, of a set of dances for orchestra. Arranged for piano.
Add. MS 14396, f.13

K.201/186a   Symphony in A major. Full score.
Lehman Deposit

K.202/186b   Symphony in D major. Full score.
Lehman Deposit

K.358/186c   Sonata in B flat major for piano duet.
Add. MS 14396, ff.22^r-29^v

K.200/189k   Symphony in C major. Full score.
Lehman Deposit

K.246 1b&2b   Cadenzas for the first and second movements of Piano Concerto in

C major.
Add. MS 61905

K.284a   Preludes for piano. Identical with the Capriccio, K.395/300g.
Cary 210

K.300   Gavotte for orchestra. Possibly a discarded movement of the ballet *Les Petits Riens*.
Koch 139

K.310/300d   Sonata in A minor for piano.
Lehman Deposit

K.371   Rondo in E flat major for horn & orchestra. Full score; the orchestration is incomplete.
Lehman Deposit

K.376/374d   Sonata in F major for violin & piano.
Cary 28

K.377/374e   Sonata in F major for violin and piano.
Zweig MS 53

K.408 n1/383e March in C major for orchestra.
Zweig MS 54

K.385   Symphony in D major ('Haffner'). Full score.
Cary 483

K.386   Rondo in A major for piano and orchestra. A fragment comprising the last 45 bars of the score.
Add. MS 32181, ff.250^r-252^v

K.387   String Quartet in G major.
Add. MS 37763, ff.1^r-13^v

K.421/417b   String Quartet in D minor.
Add. MS 37763, ff.14^r-22^v

K.428/421b   String Quartet in E flat major.
Add. MS 37763, ff.34^r-44^r

K.423-424   Duos for violin & viola.
Lehman Deposit

K.431/425b   'Misero! o sogno / Aura, che intorno spiri'. Full score; for tenor and orchestra.
Cary 412

K.426   Fugue in C minor for two pianos.
Lehman Deposit

K.447   Concerto in E flat major for horn and orchestra.
Zweig MS 55

K.458 String Quartet in B flat major.
Add. MS 37763, ff.23r-33v

K.464 String Quartet in A major.
Add. MS 37763, ff.45r-65v

K.465 String Quartet in C major.
Add. MS 37763, ff.57r-68v

K.467 Concerto in C major for piano.
Full score.
Heineman MS 266

K.476 Song, 'Das Veilchen'.
Zweig MS 56

K.485 Rondo in D major for piano.
Heineman MS 154

K.486 Der Schauspieldirektor. Full score of the Singspiel.
Cary 331

K.492 no.6 Le nozze di Figaro, 'Non so più cosa son'. Draft of the aria.
Zweig MS 57

K.492 n.6 Le nozze di Figaro, 'Non so più cosa'. Mozart's arrangement for voice, violin, and piano.
Heineman MS 157

K.493 sketches for finale of Piano Quartet in E flat major.
K.6.e.2. f.17v

K.495 Concerto in E flat major for horn. The only extant leaves of the full score (folios 13-15, 21-23).
Cary 35

K.499 String Quartet in D major.
Add. MS 37764

K.506a The 'Attwood Manuscript', with numerous corrections in Mozart's hand and two minuets composed by him.
Add. MS 58437

K.508a Eight textless canons.
K.6.e.2. f.17r

K.406/516b String Quintet in C minor.
Add. MS 31748, ff.15r-27r

K.537 Concerto in D major for piano 'Coronation'. Full score.
Heineman MS 156

K.546 Fugue in C minor for string quartet.
Add. MS 28966

K.559 Canon, 'Difficile lectu mihi Mars'
Zweig MS 58

K.559a Canon, 'O du eselhafter Peierl'
Zweig MS 58

K.570 Sonata in B flat major for piano. One leaf only of the first movement.
Add. MS 47861A, f.13

K.575 String Quartet in D major.
Add. MS 37765, ff.1r-14v

K.589 String Quartet in B-flat major.
Add. MS 37765, ff.29r-44v

K.590 String Quartet in F major.
Add. MS 37765, ff.15r-28v

K.609 Five contredanses for orcestra.
Zweig MS 59

K.614 String Quintet in E flat major.
Zweig MS 60

K.617 Quintet for armonica, flute, oboe, viola and violoncello.
Zweig MS 61

K.620 no.6 Die Zauberflöte, Priests' March. Twelve measures; the upper three string parts and flute. An earlier version of the Priests' March.
Cary 337

K.621 no.3 La clemenza di Tito - 'Deh prendi un dolce amplesso', duettino.
Zweig MS 62

K.Anh.C.16.01. Church Sonata. First violin part of a Church Sonata for 2 violins and organ in C major in the hand of Leopold Mozart. Unidentified music on the verso probably in Wolfgang's hand.
Cary 281

K.Anh. A 61/62. Zwei kleine Fugen (Versetten) für Klavier.
Cary 335

MUSIC BY OTHER COMPOSERS IN MOZART'S HAND

K.Anh. A14 Haydn, Johann Michael: Ave Maria in F major.
Add. MS 41633, ff.60r-63v

K.Anh. A52 Haydn, Johann Michael: Symphony in D major, finale.
Loan 79/6

K.Anh.A22 Reutter, Carl Georg: De profundis clamavi.
Add. MS 31748

AUTOGRAPH DOCUMENTS

'Verzeichnüss aller meiner Werke ...' (Mozart's thematic catalogue, 1784 - 91)
Zweig MS 63

Contract of marriage between Wolfgang Amadeus Mozart and Constanze Weber, Vienna, 3 August 1782.
Zweig MS 69

AUTOGRAPH LETTERS OF MOZART AND HIS FAMILY

In chronological order (to 1791)

10 November 1762 Leopold to Lorenz Hagenauer
MFC M9393.H143

14 December 1769 Mozart to his mother and sister.
Morgan MA 836

21 July 1770 Leopold to his wife.
MFC M9393.M9395

5 November 1777 Mozart to his cousin, Maria Anna Thekla Mozart.
Zweig MS 64

13 November 1777 Mozart to his cousin, Maria Anna Thekla Mozart.
Heineman MS 155

28 February 1778 Mozart to his cousin, Maria Anna Thekla
Zweig MS 65

6 July 1778 Leopold to Herr Breitkopf & Sohn in Leipzig.
MFC M9393.B835

23 September 1778 Mozart to his cousin, Maria Anna Thekla Mozart.
Zweig MS 66

10 May 1779 Mozart to his cousin, Maria Anna Thekla Mozart.
Zweig MS 67

18 June 1783 Mozart to his father.
MFC M9397.M9393

21 May 1785 Mozart to Professor Anton Klein.
Zweig MS 68

February 1786 Leopold to his daughter, Maria Anna von Berchtold zu Sonnenburg.
Add. MS 41628, ff.202r-203v

19 December 1787 Mozart to his sister, Maria Anna von Berchtold zu Sonnenburg.
Add. MS 41628, ff.204r-204v

13 April 1789 Mozart to his wife.
Heineman MS 150

25 June 1791 Mozart to his wife.
Heineman MS 151

25 June 1791 Mozart to Michael Puchberg.
MFC M9397.P977

2 July 1791 Mozart to his wife.
Heineman MS 152

INDEX